THE LAW AND CHILD LABOUR IN MALAYSIA

THE LAW AND CHILD LABOUR IN MALAYSIA

CASE STUDY IN A CHINESE NEW VILLAGE

See Hoon Peow

Pelanduk Publications

Published by
Pelanduk Publications (M) Sdn Bhd
(Co. No. 113307-W)
12 Jalan SS13/3E
Subang Jaya Industrial Estate
47500 Subang Jaya
Selangor Darul Ehsan, Malaysia.

Address all correspondence to
Pelanduk Publications (M) Sdn Bhd
P.O. Box 8265, 46785 Kelana Jaya
Selangor Darul Ehsan, Malaysia.
Website: *www.pelanduk.com*
e-mail: *rusaone@tm.net.my*

Perpustakaan Negara Malaysia   Cataloguing-in-Publication Data

See, Hoon Peow
The law and child labour in Malaysia: case study in a Chinese new village / See Hoon Peow.
Bibliography: p.163
ISBN 967-978-937-3
1. Child labour—Law and legislation—Selangor—Balakong—Case studies. I. Title.
344.595115320131

Printed and bound in Malaysia.

To my beloved wife, Keat Ching,
her love and support
is my source of strength and inspiration.

Contents

Foreword

CHILD LABOUR IS A MAJOR social problem in Third World countries. It is generally believed that its occurrence is due to widespread poverty in both rural and urban households in many of these countries. But is this the case in all parts of the world? Malaysia is seemingly more progressive than many other countries in that employers are legally prohibited, except under certain conditions, to engage children below the age of 16 in paid employment. Yet child labour is fairly common especially outside formal workplaces and in the informal sectors of the economy. The semi-urban background of Chinese new villages located at the fringes of large urban centres provides a near perfect setting for the employment of child labour. Here it becomes a genuine social issue rather than a legal problem. But why, one may ask, does child labour persist and to such an extent that it has become a social problem? Is household poverty the main cause of child labour, as conventional wisdom would have us believe? Or are there other underlying reasons that are hidden away from our view?

In this study, See Hoon Peow probes the issue of child labour in an attempt to understand the phenomenon in a semi-urban setting of a Chinese new village situated minutes away from the federal capital of Kuala Lumpur. Through his investigation, the author has uncovered fresh insights into the conditions for child labour among families whose rate of employment is high and average incomes are well above the poverty line. Yet the existence of child labour in the village challenges the legal assumption that children need protection primarily from economic exploitation. In a situation where child labour has been prompted largely by non-economic reasons, is this phenomenon a reflection of certain cultural or social factors at play? Would children who have dropped out of schools at below the legal working age be better off working, even if it is to earn some pocket money for their own entertainment and pleasure? Would child labour be a creative way to keep the child occupied and keep him out of idleness and possible delinquency? Or could it be looked upon as a partial answer to the dropout problem?

The author is to be congratulated for his investigation and for throwing new light on the reasons why children work. His findings not only deepen our understanding of child labour in Malaysia, but also contain sufficient insights to contribute to current theoretical thinking on this important subject in the wider context of the developing world.

This study in its original form was presented by the author for the degree of Masters of Philosophy at the University of Malaya. Much of the research was completed at the Centre for Malaysian Chinese Studies where the author served as an associate research fellow. As the sponsor of this study, the Centre is delighted with and endorses its publication.

Dr Voon Phin Keong
Director, Centre for Malaysian Chinese Studies
Kuala Lumpur

Preface

THE WORK PRESENTED HERE IS on my Master of Philosophy (Sociology) thesis submitted to University of Malaya in 2001. It has been substantially revised and improved. I have done some further research on related issues since then, and the findings are incorporated here.

Child labour is a widespread global phenomenon, and is often regarded as a form of child abuse or exploitation of children. Many international bodies such as the United Nations (UN) and the International Labour Organisation (ILO) have included the abolition of child labour on their agenda.

According to a report by the ILO based on statistics from about 100 countries, it was estimated that in 1995 there were 73 million children between 10 and 14 years of age in the labour force, and that in 1996 in the developing countries alone there were at least 120 million children between the ages 5 and 14 working full-time and about 250 million children of the same age category working part-time. The ILO report pointed out that sixty-one percent of these children were found in Asia.

Child labour is evidently also a common and widespread phenomenon in Malaysia. The number of children between the ages of 10 and 14 in the work force is 43,000 in the Population Census of 1980 (Department of Statistics, 1983:568) and is 39,746 in the Population Census of 1991 (Department of Statistics, 1995:485). Although there is a slight decline in the number of children in the labour force, there is no reason for us to assume that child labour would be eradicated in the near future in Malaysia.

The existence of child labour in certain places such as night markets and factories is evidence that the Children and Young Persons (Employment) Act 1966, which is the law that regulates children's participation in work activities in Malaysia, is ineffective. This study is an attempt to examine why such a law is ineffective. Poor enforcement is an obvious reason for the ineffectiveness of the law. However, the writer believes there could be other more fundamental contributing factors.

Both law and culture are forms of social control. The difference between modern law and culture is that law is backed by official sanction, while culture is enforced solely by social pressure. Sociologists of law have long noticed that culture is an important factor which influences the effectiveness of law. This is because they are the competing forms of social control. Sometimes, the laws of a society may prohibit people from behaving in a certain manner while an established cultural norm sanctions that behaviour. When law is incompatible with an established cultural norm, it is often ineffective in controlling people's behaviour. The writer believes that the incompatibility between labour law and Malaysian culture could be an important reason why our child labour law is ineffective.

The objectives of this study are:

i) to examine the influence of social and cultural factors on the practice of child labour, particularly in the Malaysian Chinese community;

ii) to look into the conditions of child work and their impact on children participating in work activities because they are important for policy making;
iii) to find ways in which the law can respond to the social and cultural factors that influence the practice of child labour.

This is important because to date there has not been any study on the influence of social and cultural factors on the practice of child labour in Malaysia.

This study is confined to the Chinese community in Malaysia due to the difficulties in conducting cross-cultural studies. The study is further limited to a Chinese new village community in the Mukim of Cheras, in the district of Hulu Langat, in the state of Selangor, Peninsular Malaysia, in the period between July 1997 and December 1997, so that an in-depth study could be conducted.

The Chinese are chosen for two reasons. First, the Chinese are known to be generally better off economically, therefore it is more likely that the Chinese child workers are not from poor families. Secondly, being Chinese himself it is easier for the writer to study the Chinese community.

It was found that child labour is very widespread in Balakong New Village. Children and young persons are engaged in various industries, doing various kinds of jobs. They are usually working under unfavourable work conditions, although many of them are paid well. Child labour often has some negative impacts on the physical, emotional and moral wellbeing of a child or young person. The writer found that poverty is not an important determinant of child labour in Balakong New Village. On the other hand, various socio-cultural factors seem to be more important determinants. Factors such as weakness in the education system, juvenile delinquency, mode of production, parental attitudes, value system and so on, seem to determine whether children and young persons work. The Malaysian child labour law, largely adapted from a western model and based on the assumption that child labour is a result of poverty, is widely violated. Even parents are willing to take the risk of violating the law by sending their children to work. They see child labour as an inevitable alternative to schooling for their children. Few other villagers are willing to report instances of child labour, even if they are aware that it is illegal. They too see no wrong in the practice.

Therefore, this study among the Chinese in Balakong New Village shows that child labour may not be a consequence of poverty. Some other factors, such as culture, education system and social environment can be important determinants of child labour.

I would like to take this opportunity to thank various people who have assisted me throughout my study, leading to publication of this book.

First of all I must thank Prof Azizah Kassim, my main supervisor, for her helpful and meticulous guidance throughout the various stage of my study. She is a great teacher and scholar. Her comments on my writing have always been precise and insightful. I learn a great deal from her. I also like to thank my co-supervisor, Ms Sharifah Suhana for her guidance in the legal aspect of my study.

I would also like to thank the following people. I must thank Dr Voon Phin Keong of the Centre for Malaysian Chinese Studies for writing the Foreword of this book. I also would like to thank Prof Abdul Hadi Zakaria of University of Malaya, he has reviewed my script and gave some good comments. I extend my appreciation to Prof Tan Chong Tin of University of Malaya, Dr Yew Yeok Kim and Dr Sothi Rachagan who have encouraged me to get my work published. I would bear all the responsibility for any shortcomings and mistakes remain in this book.

Most importantly I thank all my respondents in Balakong New Village; if not for their cooperation this study will never be possible.

Last but not least, I must thank Pelanduk Publications for publishing this book and the Centre for Malaysian Chinese Studies for the endorsement of its publication. I also wish to express my gratitude to the Centre for Malaysian Chinese Studies for giving me some financial assistance. To my family and friends who are my constant source of strength, thank you.

List of Tables

1

Introduction

CHILD LABOUR, WHICH IS A widespread global phenomenon, is often regarded as a form of child abuse or exploitation of children. Many international bodies such as the United Nations (UN) and the International Labour Organisation (ILO) have included the abolition of child labour on their agenda.

According to a report by the ILO (1996:7), based on statistics from about 100 countries, it was estimated that in 1995 there were 73 million children between 10 and 14 years of age in the labour force, and that in 1996, in the developing countries alone, there were at least 120 million children between the ages 5 and 14 working full-time and about 250 million children of the same age category working part-time. The ILO report pointed out that 61% of these children were found in Asia.

Child labour is evidently also a common and widespread phenomenon in Malaysia. The number of children between the ages of 10 and 14 in the work force was 43,000 in the Population Census of 1980 (Department of Statistics, 1983:568) and was 39,746 in the Population Census of 1991 (Department of Statistics, 1995:485). Although there is a slight decline in the number of children in the labour force, there is no reason for us to assume that child labour would cease to exist in the near future in Malaysia.

So far we have used the word "children" very loosely. Section 1A(1) of the Children and Young Persons (Employment) Act 1966 defines a child as "any person who has not completed his fourteenth year of age or of such age as the Yang di-Pertuan Agong may by notification in the *Gazette* prescribe". A young person is defined as "any person who, not being a child, has not completed his sixteenth year of age". These definitions deviate from the common definition of children. From the 17th century onwards, the age of majority is set at 21 in English Common Law. In Malaysia the age of majority was set at 18 under the Age of Majority Act 1971. However, this study has accepted the age of majority set by the Children and Young Persons (Employment) Act 1966, i.e. 17. This is to recognise that this unusual definition of age of majority may be a result of the influence of the recommendation of the International Labour Organisation to set the minimum age to enter into employment at 15 or at the age when the child completed his compulsory education. Children, or rather young persons in Malaysia completed their lower secondary education at 16 or 17, depending on the type of primary school they attended.

Perhaps it is also useful to take note of some commonly accepted definitions of child labour. The Director General of the International Labour Organisation (ILO), Blanchard (1986:1) defines child labour as follows:

> "[Child labour is] not a teenager working for a few hours to earn additional pocket money; not children

> helping on family farms; not youngsters doing household chores. But children prematurely leading adult lives, working long hours for low wages under conditions damaging to their health and to their physical and mental development, sometimes separated from opportunities that could open up for them a better future. Child labour of this kind is the object of national and international concern."

The writer accepts Blanchard's definition in principle. However, children and young persons engage in work activities directly related to their parents' occupations are also interviewed in this study. This is because the writer recognises that the situation in Malaysia may not be as clear and obvious as Blanchard puts it. In many cases, the children or young persons' activities fall into the grey area. It is difficult to determine whether they should be considered as child labour or not without close examination.

Family work is a very broad concept in the context of the Chinese culture, as the Chinese have a very complex family system. Traditionally, the Chinese lived in a corporate family, called the *jia* (家). Its members consisted of people related by descent, marriage, or adoption. "The corporate nature of the *jia* can be seen in the fact that each member belongs to one and only one *jia*, the property of the *jia* belongs to the members in common, and the income of all *jia* members is pooled to meet family need" (Sorensen, 1993:95-96). The corporate nature of the Chinese *jia* is now largely reduced and modern day Chinese in Malaysia rarely live in this type of corporate family. However, the concept "*jia*" and the obligations it entails are still very much a part of the Chinese culture. One writer accurately emphasises that *jia* is the foundation of Chinese ethic (金耀基, 1994:32) Another writer observes that even after a corporate family is separated and its members now belong to different households they often maintain very close ties financially, socially and emotionally (崔贵强, 1994:67). When one member of the *jia* is in need and if another member is in a position to help but refuses to do so, he will be strongly criticised in the Chinese community. On the other hand, membership of the *jia* is more difficult to determine, as it can be extended to various kin, which often the Chinese themselves find difficult to determine. Therefore, it is rather easy to claim that a child is fulfilling a family obligation when he works for a relative.

Childhood as a distinctive stage of human life is essentially a modern idea. Child labour was seen as a form of social problem only in the nineteenth century (Hull, 1981:48). Aries argues that the concept of childhood did not exist in Medieval Europe, and that it only came in the nineteenth century (Shipman, 1972:8). In medieval time children were portrayed as young adults and played a part in adult working and social life. "Apprenticeship started at around seven years, and among the more wealthy, children were sent into other households to learn manners, to serve and to master a trade" (Shipman, 1972:12). In pre-Industrial England, apprenticeship and domestic service were the most important means of education. Formal education became an important form of socialisation only in the nineteenth century.

In England, children under nine were prohibited from working in the factory only in 1833 and children were regarded as having rights only in 1889. Education was made compulsory in 1876 for children under ten. The Children and Young Person

Act 1933 defines a young person as between 14 and 18 years of age (Shipman, 1972:12).

Aries also argues that the spread of literacy and schooling gave rise to the idea of childhood (Shipman, 1972:8). He also asserts that attitude is a product of culture as a whole. Therefore, Bekombo (1981:113) is right to point out that child labour must be understood within individual culture. Hull (1981:47-49) points out that the negative perception of child labour in the West was affected by the working condition of a large number of children in the factories during the Industrial Revolution.

The above idea of childhood is now reflected in many international instruments against child labour. The Declaration of the Rights of the Child 1959 distinguishes "childhood" from "adulthood" and stipulates that Children should be entitled to special protection to ensure their well being. Some of the specific rights that are granted by the Declaration to children to fulfil this objective include the right to free and compulsory education, the right to opportunity for play and recreation and the right not to engage in "any occupation or employment that would prejudice his health or education, or interfere with his physical, mental or moral development". These provisions are also enshrined in the United Nations' Convention on the Rights of the Child 1989. Article 32 of the Convention recognises the right of the child for protection against economic exploitation and hazardous work, or work that interferes with the child's education, health or physical, mental, spiritual, moral, or social development. The state parties are required to take measures to provide for:

a) Minimum age or minimum ages for admission to employment;
b) Appropriate regulation of hours and conditions of employment;
c) Appropriate penalties or other sanctions to ensure the effective enforcement of Article 32.

With similar conviction, the International Labour Organisation (ILO) is committed to abolish child labour and promote compulsory education worldwide. However, ILO recognises that this will only be possible in the long run. Therefore, in the short term ILO is aiming at protecting children at work from work hazards (Bequele, 1986:14).

The Harm of Child Labour

However, work is often considered to be harmful to children. There are two research articles that deal with the risk factors of child work in Malaysia. Sinniah and Rajeswari (1993), give a general opinion from their experience as medical practitioners, of the occupational diseases that child labourers, in both agricultural and manufacturing sectors, are likely to suffer. They show the effects of work on child labourers' growth and development. These include the lack of necessary recreation, poor nutritional intake, vulnerable to diseases, and disturbance to their educational development. They then go on to point out a few "high risk" forms of child labour, among them are child prostitution, bonded child labour, begging and drug peddling. The writers claim that it is common among child labourers to have certain psychological traits. Child labourers tend to be more matured. Since they are more independent, they are more disobedient. The worrying consequences of that are that access to cash may lead the children into unhealthy activities like gambling, drinking, and more serious problems like drug addiction and sexual vices. Although, Sinniah and Rajeswari do not produce any empirical evidence to support their claims, other studies have to certain extent shown that their opinions are valid.

Mahathevan (1992) made some important discoveries when he examined a group of two hundred and ten working children. Forty of them were Malays (21%), 126 of them were Chinese (59.5%) and 44 of them Indians (21%). Although this sample is not representative of Malaysian population in terms of ethnic composition, since it is taken from many parts of Malaysia and across different industries, it is a good indication of children's work condition, in terms of geographical area and industry. He discovered that generally child labourers have a much lower health status than other children. The percentage of them being hospitalised is higher than non-working children. The difference is between 81 (38.5%) of the working children and 13 (6.2%) of the non-working children. The frequency for individual working children to be hospitalised is also higher than the non-working children, as 26 (12.3%) of the working children had one admission to hospital, 23 (10.9%) had two admissions, while 32 (15.2%) had three admissions. This is compared to 12 (93.7%) of the non-working children who had only one admission and 1 (0.5%) had two admissions. General working children require more medical care than non-working children. The writer also claims that the nutritional status of working children is also lower than that of non-working children, and that they are shorter and underweight as compared to non-working children.

Mahathevan also found the working environment of children was unsatisfactory. He discovered that 20% of the sites were too hot, 40% too noisy, and 30% had inadequate lighting.

Mahathevan also discovered that 63% of these children were subjected to ten hours or more of work, but were lowly paid (72% were paid below RM60 per month). The majority of them (62%) were only given half a day off in a week. Other studies also show similar results. In short, the present law that regulates child work is widely violated.

Child labour may also affect children's education. According to George (1992) about 20% of children enrolled in standard one in 1980 dropped out of school by 1988, i.e., before they reached the age of sixteen. She makes an assumption that these school dropouts were working. If this is so, then the effect of child labour on school dropping out rate must be taken seriously as access to education is a fundamental right guaranteed by the Universal Declaration of Human Rights. Besides, education is an important instrument to help members of the lower social class to move up the social ladder. However, she offers no indication as to whether children dropped out of school to work full-time. The writer suspects some children decided to leave school to take up full-time job. In any case this is difficult to determine. Both studies by George (1992) and Jomo and others (1992) show that the majority of child labourer's parents are lowly educated. Moreover, Jomo and others (1992) also show that a very low percentage (4%) of estate children completed secondary school, while a great majority of them (78%) dropped out of primary school of whom many became child labourers.

In short, the previous studies show that child labour is harmful but the extent of the harm is uncertain.

Causes of Child Labour

The studies of child labour are often preoccupied with the attempt to show how poor children are forced into the labour market by poverty. This is also the case in almost all the previous studies conducted in Malaysia.

Almost all authors of previous studies in Malaysia claim that poverty is the root cause of child labour in Malaysia. To some extent, child labour may be caused by poverty. However, to depict poverty as the root cause is questionable. While many studies show that child labour is widespread in poorer sections of Malaysian society, they do not explain how poverty forces children into labour. Poverty may seem to be an obvious explanation, but this can be misleading. The apparent correlation between poverty and child labour in Malaysia may be by chance. Tray (1983:452) analysed the 1976 Malaysian Family Life Survey to find that while "the common story of poor families putting children to work in order to make ends meet appears not hold [*sic*] for Malaysia: family income affect neither child labour force participation nor work hours for either age group".

Many researchers do not analyse the evidence produced in their own studies, which questions the validity of the allegation that poverty is the root cause of child labour in Malaysia. Take for example, George's (1992) study, which is the most comprehensive study so far. She collected data from both urban and rural areas. In the urban areas, places in which child labour was believed to exist were visited and the children were interviewed. Sixty-three children were interviewed and so were their parents if they were present at the sites. She admits that in the urban areas, working hours of the paid child labourer increased with the household income. However, she qualifies this trend with the fact that majority of the paid child labourers were from relatively low-income family and worked around eight to twelve hours. As a whole her findings show a mixed effect of income on hours of work done by children in her study. The rural area studied was Sabak Bernam in Selangor. This area was mainly chosen on the basis that the Education Department identified this area as having serious problems of absenteeism. Fifty children from thirty households and some of their parents were interviewed. In her analysis, she also admits that in the rural areas household income was not a factor determining the working hours of children. More importantly, she found that twelve among the fifty children did not work, while thirty-eight children worked. The non-working children were all from poor families. Six of them were from families with household income between RM350-450 per month, another four of them were from families with household income between RM500-650 per month, and the remaining two were from families with household income only between RM200-300 per month. This shows that poverty does not necessarily cause child labour. Obviously, a combination of factors would cause child labour. This makes the problem much more complicated.

However Chan (1992) argues that the household income must be analysed together with the household size. While

George did survey the households' size, she did not analyse them together with income.

Studies conducted in India (Dube, 1981) and Africa (Schildkrout, 1981; Bekombo, 1981) had shown that child labour has a unique place in these cultures.

Dube (1981:179-213) looks at the child and work as they were depicted in the Hindu culture and from there he tries to examine the cultural notions regarding the stages of human life, in doing so he places childhood and the child in its perspective. Then, he goes on to survey the patterns and extent of child labour in a few sectors to assess its place in the family and the economy. Along the way he raises some conceptual and definitional problems, together with some suggestions concerning approaches and methods in studies of child labour.

In conclusion he points out that:

> "... what is advocated is to look for deeper causes so as to grasp the nature and magnitude of children's economic contribution, and to understand the economic and cultural causes of this phenomenon."

Schildkrout (1981:81-112) conducts his studies in Kano, northern Nigeria, between 1976 and 1978, on the relationship between children's activities and the socio-economic status of their parents; on the relationship between children's roles and school attendance; and on variations in children's roles according to a number of socio-economic and cultural variables. By scanning through the daily records of children's activities he concludes that there is a clear relationship between parental income and children's activities at the extreme ends of the socio-economic scale. However, among majority of the middle-income families a range of many cultural factors intervened and influenced children's activities, independent of economic factors. He stresses that economic factors are of secondary importance except in families that barely meet subsistence needs and in families with surplus income (Schildkrout, 1981:83). On the other hand, "cultural attitudes towards childhood, the level of structural differentiation in society (i.e. whether education is a function of the family or of educational institutions), the structure and function of the family and its relation to production, the definition of adult sex roles and the sexual division of labour, are all factors which determine the pattern of children's activities" (Schildkrout, 1981:84).

Bekombo (1981:128) interestingly shows that child work is a part of the education of the African child because the African educational concept requires the participation of children in productive activities. Therefore, child labour is predominantly a western concept, and it does not applied to the African context.

In reviewing the above studies Rogers and Standing (1981:ix) pointed out that:

> "The significance of cultural factors for the mature and extent of child work is emphasised in Dube's historical review and in Bekombo's anthropological analysis, and particularly in Schildkrout's description of an integrated socio-economic system, in which children have important economic and social functions. All of these authors note the response of cultural constraints to economic change, underlining the importance of analysing culture in interaction with its socio-economic environment, and not as an independent, exogenous force."

In the present writer's opinion this may also be the case with the Chinese, as the Chinese have a set of values that acknowledge mutual responsibilities between children and adults that may encourage the practice of child labour. Therefore, child labour may also have a unique place in Chinese culture.

It may be enlightening to consider several aspects of Chinese culture, which emphasise diligence, frugality, achievement, monetary wealth and education.

The Chinese is said to possess strong work ethic, which emphasises diligence and frugality (Wu Ming Chu, 1995:167-200; 侯家驹, 1993). Therefore, the concepts of "leisure" and "play" for children are of minimal importance, if not rejected in the Chinese culture. There is a saying in Chinese that "play causes one to lose aspiration" (玩物丧志). The emphasis on "diligence" and "frugality" is often related to the belief in continuity of the family. Tai Hung-Chao (1994:11) observes that "most Chinese work diligently and live frugally for the sake of their families".

Diligence and frugality lead to accumulation of capital and the success of family enterprises, which is the dominant form of Chinese economic activity (Tai Hung-Chao, 1994:11). On the other hand, personal achievement is valued as a glory to the ancestors (Wu Ming Chu, 1995). This attitude shows the central importance of family in the Chinese culture. In turn, this shows the importance of the concept of *Xiao* (孝), which means filial piety. *Xiao* does not only regulate the relationship between the parents and the children. It is the foundation of the Chinese society. *Xiao* places obligation on the children toward parents and ancestors. In turn, parents are responsible to produce children who would glorify the ancestors. Therefore, traditionally the Chinese never thought in individualistic terms. The notion of children having rights is alien to the traditional Chinese culture. One writer even went to the extent of saying that the difference between Chinese and western culture is in the word "*Xiao*" (何子煌, 1983:32). Therefore, *Xiao* (filial piety) is the ultimate concern for the Chinese (Sim Sock Hoon, 1984; 何子煌, 1983). In other words, in Chinese culture "Obligation" is much more important than "Rights".

The Chinese also place great importance on education. However, we need to qualify this value with the class structure and social mobility in Chinese community.

A historical account of the class structure and social mobility in the Chinese community in Singapore and Malaya during 1800 to 1911 by the prominent Chinese historian Yen Ching-Hwang (1995:3-32) shows how Chinese' attitudes toward education and material wealth were interrelated. He classified the Chinese community into three classes, *shang* (商), *shih* (士) (educated elite) and *kung* (工). The *shang* class consisted of traders, shopkeepers, exporters and importers, plantation owners, property owners, financiers and tin-mining proprietors. The *shih* class consisted of clerks from foreign and Chinese firms, junior government officers, interpreters, schoolteachers and professionals. The *Kung* class consisted of artisans, shop assistants, plantation workers, mining workers and rickshaw pullers. Generally, the *shang* class occupied the top social stratum, with the *shih* class barely below them, and followed by the *kung* class.

The most interesting feature of this class system is in its mobility between classes. As Yen Ching-Hwang (1995:5) states:

> "The main characteristic of the overseas Chinese class system was its fluidity. There was no legal barrier to social mobility, nor was there a competitive examination system that people had to go through before higher status could be acquired. Wealth was the main determinant of social mobility; those who possessed it moved up the apex of the class hierarchy, and those who lost it descended even to the bottom ...In particular, movement from the upper *kung* class to the lower *shang* class was most frequent, because it was relatively easy for an artisan to change his status to become a shopkeeper. This fluidity had thus affected the shape of the classes in the overseas Chinese community.
>
> ... When the [Chinese] were overseas and congregated into a community, they naturally saw the new society structured hierarchically. They measured and graded other people according to the possession of wealth in a hierarchical order, and paid respect to those who possessed higher social status. In the process of grading other people, one could not help knowing his own status in that class hierarchy. This strong status consciousness provided an incentive for the overseas Chinese to acquire wealth and symbols of status."

The above account shows that the Chinese are very interested with the acquisition of wealth and a higher social status. Acquisition of wealth is the main objective of life for most Chinese, because it is the way towards obtaining a higher social status, which is "glorifying to the ancestors".

If it is material wealth that is valued then the Chinese will not hesitate to stop their children from school and send them to work, when it is clear that better opportunities are outside the education system. On the other hand, they may also be happy to let their children have some business experience as early as possible, so that they can have a good alternative in business if they fail to achieve in education.

Therefore, child work may be positively regarded as a good alternative to formal education, when a child's performance in education is poor. On the other hand, child work can also be considered as a good form of moral education to cultivate diligence and *xiao*.

The existence of child labour is often associated with poverty. As Swepton points out, behind the ILO policy is a belief that the root cause of child labour are economic factors and lack of effective legislation. Swepton (1986:19) proclaims:

> "Why, then, does it persist, and what is being done about it? The answer to the first question is simple: in most cases it persists because of poverty, which force families to send their children out to work or compels the children themselves to work in order to survive."

However, the present writer believes there can be a strong case against this common belief, at least in the case of Malaysian Chinese. Besides economic factors it is wise to look deeper into other social and cultural factors that may contribute to the existence of child labour.

The Present Law and Its Enforcement

There are very few articles that deal with the law regulating child labour in Malaysia and the few available ones are descriptive in nature. They only describe the provisions of the present law and its enforcement mechanism. Phillips (1979) provides a useful overview of the present law, the development of the law and its comparison with other common law jurisdictions. There are a few papers that comment on the ineffectiveness of the enforcement of the present law. However, no alternative effective legal measures have been recommended, except some "fine tuning" to the present law. Many are sceptical about the suitability of using legal measures to control child labour. One such writer, Yaqin (1996:160) states:

> "The state policy of non-interference with child labour seems to be founded on the assumption that child work has been traditionally a part of the country's social and economic patterns of life and any law imposing a total ban would not only be difficult to enforce, in its letter and spirit, but would also aggravate the problems of such families as have under (*sic*) stress of poverty to send their children to work. What a law could do was to regulate the existing patterns of child work so as to remove from the situation the possibilities of abuse and exploitation."

An official of the Labour Ministry gave the same reason against a total prohibition of child labour in an interview (Jomo, et al., 1992). The writer believes that there are a few issues that need to be considered before one can support this opinion. Firstly, we have to investigate the main cause of child labour whether it is due to poverty or culture. If the cause of child labour is poverty, the issue is whether prohibiting child labour will aggravate the problems of the poor families. This argument may not be as good as it looks, as Rodgers and Standing (1981) argue that the existence of child labour in the labour market tends to bring down the overall wage level. Therefore, child labour can only marginally improve the income level of the family. If this is a valid point, then prohibiting child labour will only create problems for the family in the short run. In the long run the absence of child labour will bring up the overall wage level. If the cause of child labour is culture, then the issue is whether a prohibition will be effective. This is a widely discussed question. Nineteenth-century sociologists of law were more negative about the possibility of using law to change culture. Now, both sociologists of law and modern legislators are more ambitious. Law is now perceived as a more independent institution, which acts upon society, and is able to regulate social behaviour freely (Cotterrell, 1984, pp.48-72).

However, in light of the wide violations discovered by previous studies, there is a reasonable consensus that the Children and Young Persons (Employment) Act 1966 is not effective in controlling child labour. The liaison officer of the Labour Department admitted that the routine inspections are not effective at all. As the employers are informed before the inspection, they can get ready for it (Mohamud, 1986). The Director of Labour, Abdul Rahim (1993:11-19), gives the following reasons for the ineffectiveness of the law and its enforcement:

1. Difficult to check on family-run establishments.
2. Child labour happens in remote areas.
3. Difficult to establish a contract of employment.
4. Lack of enforcement officers to enforce the law.
5. Difficult to talk to children to establish an employment contract.
6. Difficult to establish the age of a child or young person.
7. Children are not good witnesses.

As to the difficulty in establishing the age of the child or young person, it is difficult to see how the Director of Labour can consider this as a valid point, since we have proper Registration of births in West Malaysia.

The Director of Labour, however, has pointed out the following drawbacks in the present law. Firstly, the requirement of an employment contract places great limitation to the coverage of the law. This places many children outside the protection of the law. Secondly, the present enforcement mechanism, by way of inspections can only be effective in enforcing the law in urban areas and in the formal sectors. Besides, it is very expensive to maintain a big enforcement team.

The problem of child labour in Malaysia may not be as serious as in many developing countries. However, as the Director-General of the International Labour Organisation puts it, "There is a particular urgent need to focus on those groups of child workers who are especially vulnerable to abuse and exploitation" (Doek, 1986:7). Furthermore, there is also an urgent need to abolish work that prevent children from receiving proper education (Doek, 1986).

2

Methodology

THIS STUDY IS EXPLORATORY IN nature because this is the first attempt to study child labour and child labour law in the context of Malaysian culture. For this reason the writer adopts an anthropological perspective and bases his work on a Chinese community. This study is small in scale therefore, does not claim to be representative of the Malaysian Chinese but it can throw light on their culture and its implication to child labour. Thus, the writer is very cautious to generalise its findings.

Since there are very few studies of child labour in Malaysia, this study will rely mainly on primary data. Besides, as explained by George (1992), official data on child labour is also very limited. However, attempt is made to discover some useful secondary data from published sources. This secondary data is mainly used to provide a background to empirical data and to supplement its empirical findings.

Primary data was collected through participant observation, questionnaires and interviews. Participant's observation was conducted throughout the period of fieldwork on children and the community's activities. The writer participated as much as possible in the local activities.

From July to December 1997 the writer lived in Balakong New Village, a semi-rural community in Selangor, about thirty minutes drive from Kuala Lumpur, to conduct the fieldwork. Balakong New Village was chosen as the place to conduct fieldwork for two reasons. Firstly, it was a developing Chinese new village. The Chinese in the new villages were not so "modernised" as compared to those living in the city. Therefore, it was more likely that they still practised some traditional Chinese culture. Secondly, there were ample opportunities for the children in Balakong New Village to work, as Balakong was undergoing rapid development and is also close to Kuala Lumpur.

In the early stage of the fieldwork numerous activities in various settings were observed to discover the types of work the children did and their work places. With the co-operation of the school authority of Balakong Primary School, a survey was conducted in the school. The survey uncovered that 24 out of the total 500 students were doing some part-time work. These children were interviewed in school and asked to fill a questionnaire. Academic performances of these children were examined by looking into their report books, to determine whether working affected their academic performances.

The members of the local Lutheran church were the writer's initial key informants. They introduced the writer to various people. One of the church members, Mr Gan Yun Chong, who was a former child worker and junior gangster chief,[1] introduc-

---

[1] He was in charge of the teenage gangsters in the Hung Household gang (also known as gang 360 or 21). He was answerable to an older chief. Now, he is a committed Christian. However, he is still respected by

ed the writer to the current chief of Hung Household[2], who was his cousin. Mr Gan also accompanied the writer to interview many teenage gangsters, who are also child workers. Association with the Hung Household made it difficult for the writer to interview teenagers belonging to a rival gang in the village, the *Wah Kee*. However, the writer managed to interview some of the *Wah Kee* boys with the help of one of the *Wah Kee* boys, whom the writer managed to befriend. Later, the writer also made the acquaintance of the president of the Association of Secondary School Students, an organisation initiated by the branch of the political party MCA (Malaysian Chinese Association), and some of his friends. With their help a name list of all (225 children in total) children and young persons in Balakong New Village, between the ages 13 and 16, was produced. A list of 45 school dropouts, which included children and young persons, was also identified by their peers in the village. The president of the Association of Secondary School Students then helped and accompanied the writer to look for, and interviewed these dropouts. The writer only managed to interview 28 of these school dropouts. They were also asked to fill some questionnaires. Beside these school dropouts, another 29 part-time child workers were also interviewed and asked to fill in a questionnaire each. Some of the part-time child workers refused to co-operate.

Various people, including parents, school teachers, community leaders, and employers of children were interviewed

---

members of the Hung Household, many of whom were once under his protection.

2 Hung Household and Wah Kee are the two major gangs in Balakong New Village, and also in Malaysia.

with regard to their attitudes towards and opinions about objectives in life, education, child rearing and child work. Parents of both working and non-working children were interviewed to determine family background of the working and non-working children. All together 38 parents of working children and 22 parents of non-working children were interviewed and were asked to fill questionnaires. Two teachers were interviewed to gather information about the behaviour of the children in school. One of them had taught for more than 15 years in the local primary school. The second teacher was the disciplinary teacher of the secondary school where most of the children in Balakong New Village attended. In addition the writer interviewed two local MCA leaders, one of whom was the chief of the village, and thirty villagers chosen at random to find out their opinions on and attitudes towards child labour. No opposition party leader was interviewed, as there was no active opposition party in the village. At the supra-community level the State Assemblyman, Mr Ho Hee Lee, was interviewed to find out his opinion on and attitude towards child labour. Only two employers of child workers were willing to be interviewed.

To secure co-operation all interviews were conducted in the presence of a local villager.

The selection of the parents of non-working children was based on two criteria. Parents of children between the ages of 15 and 16 who were not working, were interviewed because majority of the children in this age group were engaged in some form of work activity. Parents of younger non-working children who had a reputation of being good students among their peers were also interviewed, as the parents' backgrounds and attitudes might be factors of these children's outstanding performance.

Children's work and other related activities were observed in their natural setting. Sometime, informal interviews with those who participated in these activities or those who had some inside knowledge about these activities were conducted. However, observation of children at work was difficult as the majority of them were not working in the village, and they were unwilling to tell exactly where they worked. Although the writer managed to observe some of the children who worked in the village, long observation was avoided as the villagers were very suspicious. The writer did not want to offend them as this could cause problems, as it was pointed out earlier that most of the teenage child workers were gangsters. The writer was also very cautious of taking photographs.

Problems Encountered

On the whole, the writer managed to have very good rapport with various people. However, there were some minor problems. The most common was meeting and interviewing the child workers themselves. Some of them might have migrated to another town, although they were in the list of dropouts. Many of these dropouts seldom stayed at home, so the writer had to meet them at the right time and place. Furthermore, some of these dropouts were inaccessible, they refused to co-operate half way through the interview. This made in-depth interview very difficult, as the writer had to make the interview quick and short so that they would not lose interest. This made it impossible to obtain some important details. Many of their parents too refused to be interviewed. Some who had agreed to an interview did not give accurate information. Very often the writer had to verify the information given with other members of the local community.

Some members of the public were unwilling to speak their mind. Both the parents of child workers and members of the public were probably affected by a misconception that any form of child labour was illegal.

Significance of Study

The United Nations and the International Labour Organisation regard child labour as a serious social problem. They are constantly devising programmes and conventions aimed at abolishing child labour for the international community to adopt. In Malaysia, our present regulations in the Children and Young Persons (Employment) Act 1966, and other policy instruments do not seem to be able to meet the problem adequately as evidenced by the large number of children engaged in work activities. However, to date there are only a few studies on the subject in Malaysia.

One of the reasons for the failure of the present socio-legal policies is the lack of understanding of the nature of the problem in the Malaysian society, in particular the Malaysian Chinese society. Child labour is often believed to be a result of poverty. No study has yet been conducted to examine the influence of culture on the existence of child labour. This study is the first attempt to study child labour and child labour law in the Malaysian cultural context.

Balakong: A Brief

The location of the study, Balakong New Village, is situated in the Mukim of Cheras in the Hulu Langat District of Selangor

Darul Ehsan, the most prosperous state in Malaysia. Balakong is situated in the vicinity of Kuala Lumpur and of the newly developed government administrative centre, Putrajaya and the Multimedia Super Corridor, Cyberjaya and other industrial areas such as Petaling Jaya, Sepang and Shah Alam. Balakong New Village is situated within a very strategic and prosperous area. This makes it a potential area for development. In the 1980s the government had declared Balakong to be an Industrial area.

The name Balakong came from the name of the river Balak, in the village. Kong is the Hakka pronunciation of the Chinese word "port" (港, *Kang* in Mandarin). This word is often used to name a settlement near a river mouth (Nyce, 1973:27). The initial residents were moved to Balakong New Village in 1950 from nearby villages, during the emergency period by the British colonial government to prevent them from getting into contact with the Malayan Communists (*Nanyang Siang Pao*, 14 October 1992). When the British government moved the initial residents to Balakong New Village they were given titles to their houses. Some of them had also applied for and were given two acres of freehold land each for agricultural purposes. Most of the initial residents plant vegetables and breed chickens and ducks for subsistence. Now, the lands given to them had been mostly developed into factory bases. Therefore, most of the residents in Balakong New Village own houses and valuable lands.

Initially, Balakong New Village was small with a population of about 1,000 and surrounded by mostly jungle. Later this jungle was developed into small rubber plantations. Since the government declared Balakong to be an industrial area in the 1980s, and allowed agricultural land to be converted into industrial land, most of the plantations have now been developed into industrial and housing estates. The value of land in Balakong has also increased tremendously. A piece of agricultural land that was worth about RM200,000 can now be sold for nearly RM2 million. This has made many in Balakong New Village millionaires (*Nanyang Siang Pao*, 11 October 1996).

The development has also attracted many people to live in this area. The population of Balakong New Village was about 5,000 in 1992 (*Nanyang Siang Pao*, 14 October 1992). While according to the Selangor Population Census of 1991 (Department of Statistics, 1995:6) the population of Hulu Langat District was 413,900. An official estimate of the population of Balakong was not available, but a local newspaper reported that the population of Balakong in 1997 was about 20,000 (*Harian Metro*, 28 October 1997). From a largely undeveloped area, with only a small community living in the midst of jungle, Balakong has now become a busy industrial and commercial centre.

Balakong New Village now has much of the necessary infrastructure. Besides basic infrastructure like electricity and water supply, Balakong New Village also has a primary school; a clinic; a church; several Chinese temples; a wet market; an assembly hall; a field and provision shops, restaurants and eating stalls. About 500 students attended the primary school. Almost all the children in Balakong New Village attended this school. What is most lacking is a police station. The nearest police station is in Cheras 11th Mile (Name of the place), which is about 15 minutes away by car. This has affected the security in the village.

Prior to industrial development, most of the residents in Balakong New Village were rubber-tapers. Now, as almost all the rubber plantations were converted into factories, many of the residents are construction and factory workers (*Nanyang Siang Pao*, 11 October 1996).

Balakong New Village is presently surrounded by seven industrial parks. Many of the houses had been converted into illegal factories inside Balakong New Village itself. The existence of these factories has brought many economic benefits as well as problems to the residents of the village.

Many job opportunities was created for the residents and job vacancies were available right at their doorsteps. Many of them are the owners of the land on which these factories are built or the owners of the factories as well. The increase in the number of factories and factory workers has caused hawking to flourish.

However, these factories also brought problems to the village. Most significant is the problem posed by foreign workers. There are so many foreign workers from Bangladesh that this place has been nicknamed by some as "Banglakong". It is believed that around 12,000 of the 20,000 residents of Balakong are foreign workers (*Harian Metro*, 28 October 1997). The large presence of foreign workers threatens the security of the village. There have been a number of robberies committed by foreign workers in this otherwise relatively peaceful community. The villagers are of the opinion that this problem is due to the lack of a police station in Balakong as alluded to earlier. Other problems faced by the villagers include floods, damaged roads and traffic congestion.

The writer believes that the increase in the number of factories has also caused more children to work (see Chapter 3).

The areas around Balakong New Village are rather urban now. However, according to Mr Hoh Hee Lee,[3] State Assemblymen for Balakong, the people in Balakong New Village are still self-contained, lack the drive to improve themselves and their village. Often, they rely on the government to solve their problems, although they can actually do much by themselves. In other words, they are not highly ambitious people. They just live their lives day by day. The reason for this attitude could be due to their low educational level, as not many residents of Balakong New Village have received more than lower secondary education.

There is only one political organisation in the village that is the local Malaysian Chinese Association (MCA) branch. There are some supporters and members of the Democratic Action Party (DAP) in the village but they are only active during the General Election period. The MCA branch has a service centre in the village. The State Assemblyman comes in every Monday to help those who need his assistance.

There is a Secondary School Students Association initiated by the MCA to encourage healthy activities among the teenagers. However, this effort is largely a failure as its activities often fail to attract the teenagers. Activities organised by the local Lutheran church are more successful, as they attracted a rather large number of teenagers to participate. However, although the church is as old as the village, it is rather marginalised, as Christianity is viewed as a foreign religion. At present the church has about fifty members. There are a few Chinese temples in the village, of which the "Stone King" (石古大王) is

[3] Personal interview on 16 November 1997.

the most important. The temple is also as old as the village. The Stone King is a local deity only found in Balakong New Village. There is a big human face looking rock at the back of the village. The initial residents believed that the rock is the guarding deity of the village, so they built the temple for the rock. On normal days there are not many worshipers in this temple, however the annual dinner to celebrate the birth of the deity is often attended by a big crowd.

3

Child Work in Balakong New Village: Extent, Categories, Types and Conditions

THIS CHAPTER PROVIDES AN OUTLINE of the different categories, types and conditions of child work found in Balakong New Village. The writer attempts to show that not all child workers are exploited or are working under hazardous conditions. Some efforts are made to distinguish the exploitative and hazardous child work from the non-exploitative and non-hazardous child work.

However, before we go into the main objective, it may be instructive to examine the extent of child labour in Balakong New Village.

The Extent of Child Labour in Balakong New Village

There are no accurate statistics on the extent of child labour in Malaysia. The situation is the same for Balakong New Village. However, there are evidences to show that child labour in Balakong can be substantial.

With the co-operation of the Association of Secondary School Students in Balakong New Village, the writer made a list of the 225 children and young persons of secondary school age, i.e. 13 years old to 16 years, in 1997. From the list, those who had already dropped out of school were identified. The result shows that 45 out of the 225 or 20% of these children and young persons had dropped out of school (see Table 1). This finding corresponds with finding of a previous study. In that study, it was found that about 20% of children enrolled in standard one in Peninsular Malaysia in 1980 dropped out of school before they completed their lower secondary education (George, 1992:18).

Table 1
Percentage and Number of School Dropouts in Balakong New Village by Age and Sex

Age	Male		Female		Total	
	%	(no.)	%	(no.)	%	(no.)
13	0.00	(0/26)	0.00	(0/26)	0.00	(0/52)
14	3.57	(1/28)	3.03	(1/33)	3.28	(2/61)
15	44.44	(16/36)	4.17	(1/24)	28.33	(17/60)
16	92.30	(24/26)	7.69	(2/26)	50.00	(26/52)
Total	35.34	(41/116)	3.67	(4/109)	20.00	(45/225)

Only 28 of these children and young persons were traceable and were interviewed. There was only one girl among them. She dropped out about one month before the writer met her, was still looking for a job. The others were employed. Therefore, we can safely assume that those who could not be traced were also doing some work.

Table 1 shows that almost all (91.11%) dropouts were boys. We can also see a trend that these students started to drop out of school when they were about 14 years old. By Form Three or

16 years of age, many boys had already left school. This trend can be explained by a combination of two factors, i.e. juvenile delinquency and poor academic performance, as shall be explained later.

The writer also conducted a survey in the Primary School in Balakong New Village (Sekolah Rendah Kebangsaan Balakong), where almost all the children in Balakong New Village and some children from the surrounding areas attended. The survey reveals that 24 (4.8%) of the 500 students worked part-time on a regular basis, from the earlier mention list, the writer's local teenage friends also identified 29 secondary school students who worked on a part-time basis regularly. The writer believes that there may be other secondary school students who worked on a part-time basis regularly that were not identified.

In total the number of full-time and part-time child workers interviewed were 79 out of the 725 (11%) children and young persons in Balakong New Village. However, the percentage of young persons (14-16 years old) who were engaged in some work activities is believed to be much higher.

From the above findings it seems that work is a common activity in many children and young persons' daily lives. This is especially true for the young persons, as only a small minority of the young persons did not engage in some work activities on a regular basis.

Classification of Child Labour's Work by Employer and Regularity

In this study child work is classified into two main categories, i.e. family work and non-family work, according to the relationship between the child worker and the person whom he or she works for.[4]

Child workers who work for their parents or close relatives are doing "family work". However, it is necessary to point out that household work is not included in this category. Only work that is directly related to income earning economic activities of the parents or close relative is considered family work. Examples of family work are children helping parents wash dishes in coffee shops or eating outlets. However, washing dishes for family at home is not family work.

Children who work for an unrelated person are engaged in "non-family work", whether or not the work is directly related to income earning activities of that person.

Both categories of child work can be sub-classified into full-time and part-time, in accordance with the children's schooling status. Children who have left school are full-time workers, and are doing "full-time work", as work is the main activities of their daily lives. They are now assumed to be responsible for their own livelihood, like an adult, although their parents may support them in time of need.

Those who were still in school but worked on a regular basis over a period of time are classified as part-time child workers. They may work in the morning before going to school in the afternoon, in the event that they are attending afternoon classes. On the other hand, they may work after school in the afternoon, if they are attending morning classes. They may also work during weekends when they are not going to school.

---

[4] The term "employer" is avoided here because many child workers may not be employed formally.

These children may work at night. Those who work occasionally, for example during school holidays are not included here, as they do not work on a regular basis.

There were two children in the sample who held two jobs. They should be treated as full-time child workers. However their second jobs were also recorded in the part-time work category. This was done mainly for the reason of convenience.

Table 2
Categories of Child Work

Family Work			**Non-Family Work**		
Full-time	10	(20%)	Full-time	18	(58%)
Part-time	40	(80%)	Part-time	13	(42%)
Total	50	(100%)	Total	31	(100%)

From Table 2, it is obvious that the majority of the child workers were doing family work. More precisely, majority of them was doing part-time family work.

Type of Job and Industry

Children in Balakong New Village were found working in various job sectors and were doing various types of work. In this section the writer tries to explain their work activities to show the inherent risks involved.

The majority of the family workers were working in small-scale factories and workshops and engaged in petty trading. The non-family workers, on the other hand, were found mainly in small-scale factories and workshops and the manufacturing and commercial sectors.

The majority of the full-time child workers were found in three sectors of jobs, i.e. the manufacturing sector, small-scale industry and the construction sector. The majority of the part-time child workers, on the other hand, were working in the small-scale industry, commercial sector and petty trading.

The manufacturing sector refers to properly licensed factories, employing a large number of workers. The small-scale factories and workshops consist of factories without proper licensing and are operating on an illegal site, and small workshops operating in shop lots, which only employ a few workers. The construction sector here includes renovation work and other work related to buildings, such as wiring, installing air conditioning and plumbing. Petty trading refers mainly to hawking businesses and food stores, which do not need high capital to operate. Although it is called petty trading, the volume of business involved may not be small. The commercial sector refers to shops and stores in shopping centres. The main difference between the commercial sector and petty trading is that the setting of the business in the commercial sector is more formal, hence less mobile and more orderly. Marginal sector refers to illegal or semi-legal activities such as theft, gambling and prostitution, and in this case attending video game centres (Rodgers and Standing, 1981:8). Minors below 18 years of age are not allowed to enter the video game centres so, attending a video game centre is an illegal activity for children. Agricultural sector here includes livestock breeding, plantation and fish rearing.

Generally, most of the child workers were found in 3 sectors, i.e. the small-scale industry, the commercial sector and petty trading. There were also a significant number of children found in the manufacturing sector. This is contrary to the common belief that child labour does not exist in the large-scale Industries. Only one child worker was found in the agricultural sector. This is consistent with the industrial developments taking place currently in Balakong. If this study had been conducted ten years ago there would probably be a larger number of child workers in the agricultural sector. This study shows that although the nation has developed substantially, the use of child labour has not been eliminated. Instead, child workers who used to work in the agricultural sector appear to have moved to the factories and the commercial sector.

Table 3 shows that in the manufacturing sector and small-scale industry child workers were mainly working in factories, small workshops and at home (cottage industry). Engineering and furniture factories were the most popular among the types of factories. In the engineering factories children were working mainly as machine operators doing a variety of jobs, such as punching holes on metals, cutting metals, and making spiral. This type of work is prohibited under the Children and Young Persons (Employment) Act 1966. Section 2(5) of the Act prohibits children and young person to manage, attend or work in proximity to machinery, as previously regulated by the Factories and Machineries Act 1967.

The writer had an opportunity to observe one of the boys at work in an illegal factory, for a short while. He was standing in front of a machine to drill a hole on a piece of metal. What he had to do was simply switch on the machine and pull down a handle. Later, he tried to make a spiral on an iron rod by using another machine. These are simple jobs; perhaps with some on-the-job training many children will be able to do it well. How-

Table 3
Distribution of Child Workers in Various Types of Work

Type of Work	Manufacturing	Small Scale Factories & Workshops	Agriculture	Commercial	Petty Trading	Construction	Marginal Activities	Total
Factory								
- Furniture		3						17
- Engineering	4	3						
- Bus Assembling	2							
- Aluminium	1	1						
- Food Production		1						
- Advertising		2						
Cottage Industry								
- Tailoring		4						13
- Packaging Erasers		1						
- Making Pencils		3						
- Making Shoes		2						
- Bottling Medicine		1						
- Making Paper Bags		2						
Workshop								
- Motorcycle Repair		3						5
- Car Accessories		2						
Construction								
- Air Condition						2		6
- Roof Drainage						1		
- Plumbing						1		
- Wiring						1		
- Laying Tiles						1		
Services								
- Shop Keeping/Sale				4				4
- Serving Beer				8				8
- Saloon				2				2
- Coffee Shop				1				1
- Hawking					22			22
- Agriculture			1					1
- Clerk	1							1
Marginal Activity								
- Attending Video Game Centre							1	1
Total	8	28	1	16	22	6	1	81

Note: There were two full-time child workers, who also work part-time, and they are recorded twice. Hence, the higher number of child workers than the number interviewed, i.e. 79.

ever, after long hours of work, when one is tired and concentration declines, accidents can happen.

In the furniture factories, child workers operated machines to drill holes, and to cut wood. Sometimes, they assembled furniture. Woodcutting is a particularly dangerous job. If the person who handles the machine is not careful, he runs the risk of having his fingers cut off. This is especially dangerous for children as they are normally less disciplined. This had happened to one of the boys that the writer interviewed, who was once working in a furniture factory. The wood cutting machine cut off portions of his fingers on his right hand. Often, child workers were also wounded by the air gun that they used to punch nails.

Other factories where child workers were found included those producing aluminium products, food and advertisement boards. There were also two child workers working in a bus-assembling factory. Child workers in these factories were doing similar work as the child workers in the engineering and furniture factories. Nevertheless, it is worth noting that the child workers in factories producing aluminium products like door gates and lampposts and also did some welding, which could be dangerous if proper safety equipment was not used properly. The writer saw one boy welding parts of a door gate. He did use a goggle. Child workers who worked in factories producing advertisement boards also participated in paint spraying and fixing the advertisement boards. Long-term exposure to paint spraying can cause chemical poisoning, neurological impairment, dermatitis, lead poisoning and so on. Fixing advertisement boards requires the child workers to climb high, thus running the risk of falling from heights.

There were five boys who worked in motorcycle and car accessories workshops. These boys were rather skilled. One of them told the writer that he always wanted to work in a motorcycle workshop. Apparently, this is due to his interest in motorcycle racing. The writer was told that he was one of the best racers in illegal motorcycle racing in the Kajang area. He was so good and his motorcycle so well modified that many people dare not race with him. The writer also observed another 16-year-old boy, who was always left in charge of the motorcycle repair workshop alone. The owner of the motorcycle repair workshop, the boy's brother, very seldom come to the workshop. Yet another boy, who helped his father in a motorcycle repair workshop after school, repaired the writer's motorcycle without assistance from his father. The writer also observed a boy who worked in a car accessories workshop fixed a radio in a car successfully without any assistance. Another boy who also worked in a car accessories workshop told the writer that the work was easy and enjoyable. Although, these boys learned a lot of useful skills in these workshops, their work required them to stay in harmful postures, such as squatting for a long period of time. This may have detrimental effects on their physical development.

The majority of the part-time family workers were found in petty trading and cottage industries. "Cottage industry" here refers to industrial work that was done at home. Some factories around the village contracted out some work to the villagers to be done at home. These include making mechanical pencils, shoes, paper bags, packaging rubber erasers and tailoring. When a member of the family became a contractor, other members of the family, including children would help with the work. These children work at home alongside other family members, without a fixed schedule.

They worked as they were watching television or talking to each other. Since they worked alongside their family members, it is rather like a family gathering and entertainment. They did not think that they were working but rather they were helping their family member.

The greatest numbers of child workers were found in petty trading. Petty trading refers mainly to operating hawker stalls. Petty trading is a very common type of trade in Asia. It can take various forms, such as:

> "Street vendors selling fruits, clothing, trinkets, in market places crowded with tiny stalls or with their produce simply set put on the ground. Little booths or carts are strung out along sidewalks or clustered around bus and train stations selling every variety of local cooked foods and drinks." (Clammer, 1993:169)

Children in Balakong New Village were found helping their parents or relatives to sell a wide variety of products. Normally, they worked alongside their parents or relatives to serve food or drinks on the table, to pack things or simply to mind the stall when their parents or relatives were busy doing something else. Interestingly one eleven-year-old girl's job was rather demanding for someone her age. She did not go to the market with her parents to sell chicken; rather she stayed at home to take orders from customers through the telephone. When someone called, she would take down the person's name, the amount and the specifications of the kind of chicken wanted. When her parents returned home, they would look into the order and despatch the chicken to the customers. She seemed to be very well versed in her job. She could describe the process and the specifications of the types of chicken in detail, which the writer found hard to memorise.

Some of these so called petty trading or hawking were not petty at all. Certainly the business of the parents of the girl mentioned above was not small. One parent said that he could earn up to RM10,000 per month, although it was not clear whether he was referring to profit or turnover of his business. However, as he was living in a big and elegantly renovated brick house, he would have been well to do.

A group of boys were found working in the construction sector. They were doing work like plumbing, installing gutters and air conditioners on the roof, wiring and laying tiles. All these are hazardous work, as these children were required to climb high on the roof, thus running the risk of falling down. The boy who worked as an electrician was exposed to the risk of experiencing electrical shock. The boy who laid tiles showed the writer his hands, which were burned by lime. As shall be discussed in detail in Chapter 6, one boy fell from the roof and sustained serious injuries.

It was also interesting to note that although these were dangerous works, many of them were full-time family child workers who worked for their parents or relatives. This showed that family child workers might not be as safe as it was believed to be.

A group of eight girls, between the age 15 and 16, were hired by a large beer company, to serve beer on special occasions such as wedding dinners. The writer had an opportunity to observe them during a wedding dinner, which the writer attended. They were in uniform, and walked around to serve the guests with beer when they were asked to do so. The dinner began at 7.30pm and finished at around 10pm.

This is another example of children hired by a multinational corporation. This was not unknown in Malaysia, as in 1994 there was a report in the local dailies about a multinational electronic factory which was found guilty of employing 65 children (*Sin Chew Jit Poh*, 15 December 1994).

The rest of the child workers who worked in the comercial sector were found working in shopping centres, retail shops, coffee shops and hairdressing salons. In the shopping centres and retail shops they were normally engaged as sales persons. In coffee shops, they served food and drinks. The two girls who worked in a hairdressing salon were only "shampoo girls" who washed customer's hair, as they had yet to learn the hair-cutting skill.

Only one boy was found working in the agricultural sector. He helped his father to breed ducks. He helped to feed the ducks and to send the ducks back to their hutch.

Another boy was working for his brother as a video game centre attendant. His main function was to manage the centre and to change coins. However, in this video game centre gambling activities were carried out. According to Malaysian regulation only those who were 18 and above could enter a video game centre. Therefore, his presence there was illegal, so was his employment. However, he was not the only one who worked in video game centre. There were two other boys who were once working in a video game centre for a short period before they found other jobs. However, the case of this video game centre keeper showed once again that family work might not be harmless for children.

Finally, there was a 16-year-old girl who worked as a clerk in an engineering factory owned by an unrelated person. She was the only white-collar child labour in the sample.

In short, children and young persons were found working in various job sectors and in various types of employment. While the work experience might be good training for them, their work might have detrimental effects on them as shall be discussed in detail in Chapter 6.

Gender Division of Child Work

It is often reported that boys and girls are normally engaged in different kinds of work. This is the result of different perceptions on the two sexes. Normally, boys are preferred in more physical demanding jobs while girls normally worked at home.

Generally, this gender division is also visible in Balakong New Village. All the children who were employed in factories and small workshops were boys, except for one girl who worked as a clerk in a factory. Factory and workshop works are physically more demanding as described in the above section. Girls were found in petty trading, cottage industry and the commercial sector. Although some boys also worked in these sectors, they were normally younger and were working on part-time basis.

Working Conditions

The working conditions of the child workers in Balakong New Village shall be discussed in this section. Conditions that shall be analysed include days of work in a week, hours of work in a day and wages of the child workers. A comparison will be made between the working condition of family child workers and the non-family child workers and those working full-time and part-time.

Working Conditions of the Full-time Child Workers

Generally, all the child workers worked more days in a week than a normal white-collar worker in Malaysia. The white-collar workers in Malaysia normally work five and a half days in a week. The average number of working days of the full-time family child workers was 6.3 days in a week. While, the average number of working days of the full-time non-family child workers was 6.25 days in a week. Therefore, the full-time family child workers generally worked slightly more days in a week than the full-time non-family child workers.

Table 4 shows that children employed on full-time basis worked at least 6 days a week. There were 3 full-time family child workers and 4 full-time non-family child workers who worked 7 days in a week. Some of those working 7 days a week worked for a shorter period on Sunday. One boy said he had only two days off in a month.

Table 4
Number of Working Days per Week

Category	6 Days	7 Days	6/7 Days	Total
Full-time Family Work	7	3	0	10
Full-time Non-Family Work	13	4	1	18
Total	20	7	1	28

Besides working for many days per week the child workers also had long working hours per day. Table 5 shows that all children, except one, had to work for eight or more hours per day. Forty-four percent of these children had to work for 10 hours or more. The longest working period was 12 hours per day. This involved the boy working at the video game centre. He managed the video game centre from 8am to 5pm, and then rested for a while before taking up another job in making shoes for another three hours. Both his employers were his relatives.

Table 5
Number of Working Hours per Day

Hours	Full-time Family Work	Full-time Non-Family Work	Total	
7½		1	1	(3.6%)
8		1	1	(3.6%)
8½	2		2	(7.1%)
9	2	7	9	(32.1%)
9½	1	1	2	(7.1%)
10	2	3	5	(17.9%)
10½		4	4	(14.29%)
11			0	
11½	2	1	3	(10.7%)
12	1		1	(3.6%)
Total	10	18	28	(100%)

One of the boys who worked 11½ hours per day was working in a motorcycle repair workshop. The second worked as a plumber and the third worked in a furniture factory. The two boys who worked in the motorcycle repair workshop and as plumber were also family workers. The mode number of hours children worked was 9 hours. The mean number of hours children worked was 9 hours 36 minutes. This was well beyond the six hours for children and seven hours for young persons permitted by the Children and Young Persons (Employment) Act 1966.

Non-family workers were in a more favourable condition than the full-time family child workers as far as working hours were concerned. As indicated above most of those who worked the longest hours per day were family workers. More family workers were also found working for longer hours. The mean hours of work for the family workers were 9 hours 57 minutes. This was slightly more than the non-family workers whose mean working hours was 9 hours 30 minutes.

Most of these full-time child workers were given one-hour lunch break and about 15 minutes break for tea. However, the full-time family child workers and those who worked in small workshops generally get a shorter lunch break. They had to finish their lunch as fast as possible and go back to work. This is probably due to the nature of the job and the nature of the relationship between the employer and the worker. The full-time family child workers who were members of the family were expected to work harder for the success of the family enterprise. The nature of the work in a small workshop is that it cannot run on a fixed schedule. When there was more work on a particular day then the workers would have to work harder. When there was less work they could relax.

All the full-time child workers, regardless whether they worked for family or not, received a monthly payment. Table 6 shows that the majority of them received between RM500 to RM899 per month. Only two children received less than RM500 per month. Three children received RM900 and more. The highest paid boy received about RM1,200 per month. He was working for a company owned by his relative who had businesses in a few Southeast Asian countries i.e. Indonesia, Thailand and Singapore. This company dealt with air ventilation system. He helped to install the ventilation system on the house roof. He worked seven days a week and ten hours per day. Sometimes he was sent to the other Southeast Asian countries to work.

Table 6
Wages of Full-time Child Workers

Pay (RM)	Family Work	Non-Family Work	Total
300-399	1		1
400-499	1		1
500-599	2	5	7
600-699	2	5	7
700-799	2	2	4
800-899	1	4	5
900-999		1	1
1000-1099		1	1
1100-1199			
1200-1299	1		1
Total	10	18	28

Number of Full-time Workers: 28

However, all the child workers were not given any fringe benefits. This was the result of legal regulation. Both the employers and the child workers assumed child work was illegal (in fact it was not always illegal). Therefore, employers did not give fringe benefits and child workers did not insist on them. Parents too perceived child work in a similar manner.

In general, children who were engaged in non-family work received higher pay than children engaged in family work. The mean pay of the non-family workers was RM670.58 per month, while the mean pay of family workers was only RM645 per month. However, both the lowest paid child and the highest paid child were working for family members. However, the norm was as shown in Table 6, i.e. the non-family child workers consistently receiving slightly higher pay than the family workers.

It is interesting to note that the working conditions and income of child workers in Balakong New Village differed from what people commonly believed. Firstly, contrary to the common belief full-time family child workers were not working under better working conditions. This was probably the result of the influence of Chinese culture. As a member of the family the full-time family child workers were probably expected to work harder but received less pay for two reasons. As a member of the family they had a moral obligation to contribute to the success of the family enterprise, thus showing their *xiao*. Working hard was also part of their training. Hence the emphasis is on diligence. On the other hand, the unrelated employers have no interest in other people's children's upbringing and tend to assert less authority on the full-time non-family child workers.

Secondly, the full-time child workers were actually receiving quite good pay, taking into consideration their age, lack of work experience and low qualification. This was probably why, although they worked very hard, only two of them say they did not like their employers. However, the children do not give clear reasons why they did not like their employers.

Working Conditions of the Part-time Child Workers

The working conditions of the part-time child workers were more varied as compared to those of the full-time workers. To a great extent the working conditions of the part-time child workers were very much determined by the nature of the work they engaged in. Their relationship with their employers also had some influence over their working conditions. Therefore, we could expect a difference between the working conditions of the part-time family child workers and that of the part-time non-family child workers.

Table 7 shows that some children only worked as little as one day a week, but some had to work as many as seven days. Many children only worked during weekends when they were not attending school. Those who worked during weekdays normally did their work either after or before school, depending on whether they were attending morning or afternoon classes. Some of them worked at night regardless whether they attended morning or afternoon classes. Two boys who worked full-time worked on their second job at night after they finished their main job. The first boy as alluded to earlier worked as video game centre attendant during the day and helped his parents to make shoes at night. The other boy worked in a shop that sells air conditioners during the day and helped his parents in a restaurant at night.

Nevertheless, about 30% of the family workers and 15% of the non-family workers worked for more than 4 days a week. As for those whose working days were irregular, it all depends on the availability of work. Most of the family workers who did not work on a regular basis were in the cottage industry. While most of the non-family workers who did not work on a regular basis were the girls who served beer. The nature of the cottage industry is that the workload depends on whether the main factory receives any order and whether the main factory can adequately handle the order. For the girls who served beer their availability of work depends on whether there were any special functions, parties, wedding dinners and so on.

Table 7
Part-time Child Workers: Number of Workdays per Week

	Days								
Category	**1**	**2**	**3**	**4**	**5**	**6**	**7**	**Irregular**	**Total**
Family Work	3	15	3	0	2	8	3	6	40
Non-Family Work	0	3	0	0	1	1	0	8	13
Total	3	18	3	0	3	9	3	14	53

Those who only worked during the weekends usually worked with hawkers. The majority of them were family workers. The hawking business during the weekends is normally much better than the weekdays. The children do not have to attend classes during the weekends and their parents are too busy at that time to keep an eye on them, therefore the better alternative is to bring them to help in their work.

If we look at the number of hours these children worked in a day we can see that many of those who only worked during weekends were working for long hours at a stretch. But some of those who worked for more than 4 days only work for one or two hours a day. Nevertheless there were those who worked for many days and long hours.

As shown in Table 8 the mode working hours of the part-time child workers is 3 hours. However, more than 50% of them worked for 4 hours or more a day. The majority of those who worked for more than 4 hours per day were again family workers. Therefore, family workers not only worked for more days in a week, they also worked for longer hours per day. This finding disproved the common belief that family workers are less exploited. Those who had long working hours per day were normally found in petty trading and the commercial sector. Their work required them to help mind the shop or the stall for long hours. While those who worked at home, i.e. in the cottage industry, worked for shorter hours as they could stop as and when they were tired or bored.

Table 8
Part-time Child Workers: Number of Working Hour per Day

Hours	Family Work	Non-Family Work	Total
1	4		4
2	4		4
3	9	8	17
4	7	2	9
5	5		5
6	3		3
7	4	1	5
8			0
9	1		1
10		1	1
11	1	1	2
12	1		1
Irregular	1		1
Total	40	13	53

The majority of the part-time child workers were not given a break during their working hours as many of them only worked for a few hours. Nevertheless, some of those who worked for long hours were given a short break.

Part-time family work was usually referred to as "unpaid family work". However, Table 8 shows that this phrase is not an accurate description of the actual situation. As indicated in the table, only ten children did not receive any payment for their work. The others received some form of wages. Some of them were paid very little while others were paid a substantial sum.

Table 9 reveals that the method of calculating pay varies. Some of them were paid a monthly salary like the full-time workers. Others were paid on piece rate basis. Yet some were paid on a daily basis. Only one was paid by the hour.

Table 9
Part-time Child Work: Methods of Calculating Pay

Category	Hourly	Daily	Monthly	Piece rate	No Pay	Total
Part-time Family Work		16	8	6	10	40
Part-time Non-Family Work	1	11	1			13
Total	1	27	9	6	10	53

Although it is possible to relate the method of calculating pay with the type of work children do, sometimes the method of calculating pay also varies for children doing the same type of work. For example only those who were found in the cottage industry were paid on a piece rate basis. However, arrangements were also made to pay the children on a daily basis. Those who were in the commercial sector were usually paid on a daily basis; those who had a fixed work schedule (e.g. working from Monday to Friday, 4pm to 10pm) were paid monthly. Normally children engaged in petty trading were paid either on a daily or monthly basis.

Those who were paid monthly received around RM10 to RM300 per month. Those who were older were paid more. Some of those who were paid on a daily basis only received as little as RM1 per day but some received as much as RM25. However, the part-time non-family workers earned more than the family workers. The highest pay a non-family worker received was RM30 per day. She worked for two days a week and 11 hours a day. The girls who served beer received RM25 for a three-hour job, but sometimes with overtime allowance they could earn as much as RM50 per day. The highest pay for family workers was RM20 per day. However, 22.5% (i.e. 9 persons) of the part-time family workers received less than RM10 per day, while 25% of the part-time family workers were not paid a salary.

The basis for payment on piece rate was as follows:

a) 17 sen per pencil made;
b) RM5 per 1000 erasers packed;
c) RM5 for 5 pieces of cloth cut;
d) 2.5 sen per paper bag made.

On the average, 7 persons (adults and children) can make around 3,000 pencils a day. Therefore, they can earn about RM70 per day each. Those who made paper bags said that they earned around RM20 per month. A boy who helped his sister to pack erasers said that the latter paid him RM50 per month.

It should be pointed out that while there were no significant differences between the working days and working hours of the part-time family workers and the part-time non-family workers, the non-family workers often received higher wages. Here again, we may be seeing the influence of Chinese culture on child work. Parents or close relatives did not think that the young family members were working for them. These children were only "helping" them, therefore the wages given were only tokens of appreciation or a means to attract the children to "help". On the other hand, if children were hired by non-family members, they were considered "working"; therefore demanded a fair market rate. Schildkrout (1981:101), therefore, is right when he points out that "a child worker, working for wages in a wage economy, is a worker who happens to be a child. A child who works in a familial context is a child who happens to work."

Generally, the relationship between these part-time child workers and their employers, whether related or not, was good. Only two part-time non-family child workers said they were not sure whether they liked their employers because sometimes their employers scolded them for their mistakes at work.

In short, the non-family workers were working under a slightly more favourable condition than the part-time family child workers. This was a result of their status as a "worker" rather than a "helping hand".

Age and Work History

The majority of the child workers in the sample were between the ages 15 and 16 (see Table 10). According to the Children and Young Persons (Employment) Act 1966 they are categorised as "young persons". Therefore, the authority needs only to stop them from engaging in work activities for one or two years before they reach the legal age of 17 years.

Table 10
Age of Child Workers

Age	Family Work	Non-Family Work	Total
9	4	0	4
10	1	0	1
11	8	0	8
12	11	0	11
13	4	0	4
14	0	2	2
15	11	15	26
16	9	14	23
Total	48	31	79

Table 10 also shows that the non-family workers were older than the family workers. The mean age of the non-family workers is 15, while the mean age of the family workers is 13. However, the mean age of all the child workers is 14. The family workers were younger mainly because they were made to start work activities at a much younger age than the non-family workers. However, the majority of the younger child workers were part-time family child workers (see Table 11).

This finding is similar to the finding of Lai's (1992:115) study, which was conducted mainly among the Chinese in the urban area of Penang. In comparison the majority of the child workers in both Mahathevan and Paul Chan's studies were 14 years old. The age structure of the child workers in this study is very likely to be an accurate reflection of the actual age structure of Chinese child workers in Malaysia.

The work history of these children shows that children in different categories of work began working at different ages. Generally, the part-time family workers begin to work at a much lower age than the full-time non-family workers do. The mean age when the part-time family workers began to work is 10, and the mode age is 11. On the other hand, the mean age when the full-time non-family workers began to work is 14, and the mode age is 15. The mean ages when the full-time family workers and the part-time non-family workers began to work are both 13. Majority of the child workers began to work before the age of 14. While the part-time family child workers began to work as young as six years old. This indicates that there are probably different reasons why children worked. (See details in Chapter 4)

Table 11
The Age Children Began Working by Category of Work

	Full-time Workers		Part-time Workers		
Age	Non-Family Work	Family Work	Non-Family Work	Family Work	Total
6				3	3
7				2	2
8			1	4	5
9		1	1	5	7
10				3	3
11	1			11	12
12			2	2	4
13	4	2	2	4	12
14	4	3	1	2	10
15	8	3	4	1	16
16	1	1	2	1	5
Total	18	10	13	38	79

At what age children begin working depends on their reasons for working and who decides whether they should work or not. For the full-time and the part-time non-family child workers, in many instances it is the children who chose to work. In the case of the part-time family child workers however, it is their parents or their relatives who decided for them. Normally when children grow older they become more independent. (See details in Chapter 4)

Many Chinese see child work as a form of apprenticeship or as an alternative to schooling. However, whether this is so in practice depends very much on whether the child workers stayed in one occupation for a long enough period for them to acquire enough skills. This is especially important for the full-time child workers.

This study found that about 40% of the full-time child workers in the sample had engaged in at least two types of job. The majority of those who had never changed their jobs were those who started working not long ago. Only a very small group of the full-time child workers stick to the same type of job when they changed employers. Therefore, if this phenomenon persists, then child labour will never be an effective alternative to schooling.

The part-time non-family child workers changed their jobs very frequently. Whenever a better offer came along they would change their jobs. The part-time family child workers, on the other hand, normally stayed in one job because they worked for their parents or relatives.

Pay Utilisation

Most of these children used a large proportion of their pay for themselves. As shown in Table 12 only a few of them give part of their pay to their parents.

Most full-time child workers gave part of their pay to their parents every month. This indicates that they were treated like an adult who is expected to make financial contribution to their family. Generally, they gave around RM100 to RM300 per month to their parents. They used the rest of their pay for themselves. There were a few full-time family workers, who handed over all or a large part of their pay to their parents for safekeeping.

Table 12
Frequency of Children Giving Money to Parents

	Full-time		Part-time		
Frequency	**Non-Family Work**	**Family Work**	**Non-Family Work**	**Family Work**	**Total**
Every Month	16	7	3	2	28
Often		1	1		2
Sometime	1		4		5
Not Often			2		2
Never	1	2	3	36	42
Total	18	10	13	38	79

The part-time non-family workers had more control over their pay. They had more freedom whether to give their money to the parents or not. As they were still in school, there was no expectation that they should contribute to their family financially. As for the part-time family workers, since they normally receive their pay from their parents, it is only logical that a majority of them do not give their money back to their parents. However, there were two part-time family child workers who chose to give their money back to their parents for safekeeping.

Many of these children said they saved part of their pay and spent the rest on things that they wanted, such as clothes and entertainment. The older girls like shopping in big shopping centres like the Mines Shopping Centre near Balakong. The older boys, on the other hand, spent their money on their motorcycles and on girls. Many of them owned motorcycles, and they had to spend some money maintaining, decorating and modifying them so that the vehicles would be more powerful. They also went to places like Karaoke bars and discos with girls, and very often they had to pay for the girls accompanying them. Quite often they gambled in the video game centres and many of them lost a lot of money there. Some of the full-time workers very often overspent, and had to request back their money from their parents. As for the part-time workers, they continued asking money from their parents. Therefore, in reality giving money to parents is like a formality. In the end parents often do not have the opportunity to spend their children's money.

Summary

Child labour is common in Balakong New Village, even though the village was a prosperous one. Children were found working in various job sectors, doing various types of work. Although these children were clearly not "cheap labour", they were working under tough conditions. Many of them were required to perform dangerous tasks, worked for long hours and for many days per week.

Although it was commonly believed that family child workers were in an advantageous position in comparison to the non-family child workers, the Balakong New Village case study showed that they are not. Children working with family members often worked under tougher conditions than the children working with non-family employers. The majority of these child workers had no career plan for themselves. They spent a large part of their money freely.

4

Poverty as a Determinant of Child Labour

Introduction

TO DATE THERE IS STILL no study pointing convincingly to the causes of child labour in Malaysia. Almost all the previous studies in Malaysia were overwhelmed by the effort to show that poverty, which many international organisations such as the United Nations (UN) and International Labour Organisation (ILO) believe to be the cause of child labour, is also the cause of child labour in Malaysia. These studies only manage to show that child workers normally came from relatively poorer families. However, the fact that child workers came from a poorer background does not necessarily mean child labour is caused by poverty. If poverty is the cause, why is it that some poor families as in George's study (1992), did not send their children to work while others did?

The fact that child workers come from certain demographic and family backgrounds is often said to indicate that poverty is the root cause of child labour. It is often shown that child workers were normally the older children of big families with low household income, their parents were of older age, lowly educated, with blue-collar occupations.

In this chapter the writer tries to examine whether these demographic and family characteristics apply to the child workers in Balakong New Village. Some of the demographic and family backgrounds of the child workers will also be compared with that of a sample of non-working children in Balakong New Village. This is done to ascertain whether poverty is the cause of child labour in Balakong New Village.

Family Size

It is generally believed that most child workers were from large families. Given the background of large families with low income, it is believed that many families would have to "expel" some children out to work, to bring some income to the family (Jomo (ed.), 1992). Most of the previous studies indicate the family size of the child workers to be between 7 to 10 members. However, results of this study to some extent challenge this common belief. The majority of the child workers did not come from very big families. Twenty-six (32.9%) of them came from families with 4 children. Another 26 of them came from families with less than 4 children. The rest of them, 25 (31.65%) in total, came from families with more than 4 children. The mode number of children per family was 4. Generally, 68.35% of the child workers were from families with 4 or less than 4 children. (See Table 13)

More family child workers were from smaller families. About 40% of the family child workers were from families of less than 4 children, compared to 30% of the non-family child workers. However, the difference is not significant, because the mode number of children per family for both categories of child workers was 4. Furthermore, 68% of either the family child workers or the non-family child workers were from families with 4 children or less than 4 children.

Table 13
Number of Children in Child Workers' Families according to Work Category

Number of Children per Family	Non-Family Work	Family Work	Total
1	1	0	1 (1%)
2	1	7	8 (10%)
3	7	12	19 (24%)
4	12	14	26 (33%)
5	5	11	16 (20%)
6	4	0	4 (5%)
7	1	4	5 (6%)
Total	31	48	79 (100%)

It is important to stress that a high proportion of these child workers did not come from big families. If we were to compare the family size of the working children with the family size of twenty-two non-working children, the former seems to be slightly larger. Table 14 shows that about 64% of the non-working children came from families with less than 4 children, about 27% of non-working children came from families with 4 children and only about 10% of the non-working children came from families of more than 4 children. The mode and mean number of children per family for the non-working children were 3 and 3.35. There seems to be a correlation between family size and children's participation in work activities. However, although the child workers had a bigger family size than the non-working children, they were not from large families.

Table 14
Number of Children in Non-Working Children's Families

Number of Children per Family	Non-Working Children	
1	0	
2	3	(13.64%)
3	11	(50%)
4	6	(27.27%)
5	2	(9.09%)
Total	22	(100%)

Apart from poverty, the correlation can be explained by referring to other factors such as parents' level of education. The more educated parents tend to have fewer children and also more likely to disagree with child labour, as shall be explained later.

Birth Order

It is commonly believed that the older children in a poor family will have to work to sustain their younger siblings. Table 15 shows that majority of the child labour in this sample were the older siblings, and those ranked first, second and third, in their respective families. However, this can be misleading. We have seen in previous section that majority of these children were from small families. Many of those ranked first among their siblings came from families of two children, many of those ranked second came from families of three children and many of those ranked third came from families of four children. Besides, if we put them into their particular category of child work, only the part-time workers were the "older" siblings in the families. This pattern in part-time family work can be explained with the requirement for the older children to set a good example for their younger siblings; to help their parents is an expression of *xiao*. The majority of the full-time workers were the youngest siblings in the families. This may have something to do with juvenile delinquency, as shall be explained later.

Table 15
Birth Order

	Full-time		Part-time		
Birth Order	**Non-Family Work**	**Family Work**	**Non-Family Work**	**Family Work**	**Total**
First	3	1	4	11	19
Second	5	1	5	9	20
Third		2	2	9	13
Fourth	2		2	2	4
Fifth		1			2
Sixth				1	1
Youngest	8	5		6	17
Total	18	10	13	38	79

This pattern again indicates that poverty may not be the only explanation of the incidence of child labour. There could be other more important determinants. If we look at the full-time child workers who were between 15 to 16 years old, they had older brothers or sisters who were no longer in school, and were working. These elder siblings were in a position to help their family financially, and there was no need for their youngest brothers to work to sustain the families.

Parents' Age

The parents of the child workers in this study were slightly younger compared to the parents of the child workers in George's study. In her study more than 50% of the parents in the urban samples were less than 49 years of age, while more than 50% of the fathers in the rural samples were more than 49 years of age and more than 50% of the mothers were less than 44 years of age.

Table 16 shows that 60.5% of the fathers and 89.47% of the mothers of the child workers in this study were less than 49 years of age. This age structure is similar to the age structure of the parents in the urban samples in the study by George (1992).

Table 16
Age Distribution of Parents

Age Group	Fathers of Working Children (N = 38)	Mothers of Working Children (N = 38)	Fathers of Non-Working Children (N = 22)	Mothers of Non-Working Children (N = 22)
30-34		3		1
35-39	4	8	4	8
40-44	12	13	8	10
45-49	7	10	7	2
50-54	8	3	2	1
55-59	3		1	
60 and Above	2			
Deceased	2			
Not Available		1		

George believes that the age structure of the parents in the urban area shows that the middle-aged parents' productivity had declined. Therefore, children were required to make contribution to the family. However, the writer believes this is not a valid explanation of the participation of children in work activities in Balakong New Village. Given that 42% of the fathers and 63% of the mothers were less than 44 years of age, it is unlikely that they were not productive anymore. Furthermore, it should be borne in mind that many of the children started work activities a few years ago when their parents were even younger and probably at the peak of their career. Moreover, given the impressive economic development in Malaysia in the past 10 years and that there were ample employment opportunity in Balakong, it is difficult to imagine that these parents were poor, if they were willing to work and able to do so.

However, the parents of the working children were older as compared with the parents of the non-working children. About 86% of the fathers and about 95% of the mothers of the non-working children were less than 49 years of age. In comparison, 55% of the fathers and 86% of the mothers of the non-working children were less than 44 years of age.

This difference in age, together with other factors may have a bearing on the value system, attitudes and outlook of these two groups of parents, which would be discussed later in the next chapter.

Parents' Education Background

Generally, a person's educational background is a good indicator of his attitudes and social status. Table 17 shows that the majority of parents of child workers were not highly educated. More than 50% of them had only primary education, while a few mothers had never received any formal education. Except for two fathers, all of them had Chinese medium education. This educational background indicates that these parents were greatly influenced by traditional Chinese culture. It may also indicate that they were conservative in their attitudes.

The parents of the non-working children were more influenced by non-Chinese culture, as they were more educated; and a slightly higher percentage of them had their education in mediums other than Chinese (See Table 18).

From Table 17 we can also see some correlation between parent's levels of education and children's work. It looks like children who have parents with lower level of education are more likely to engage in child work.

Table 17
Educational Attainment of Parents

Level of Education	Fathers of Working Children (N = 38)	Mothers of Working Children (N = 38)	Fathers of Non-Working Children (N = 22)	Mothers of Non-Working Children (N = 22)
No Formal Education		4 (10.53%)		
Primary	20 (52.63%)	27 (71.05%)	7 (31.81%)	13 (59.09%)
Secondary	16 (42.11%)	7 (18.42%)	13 (59.09%)	8 (36.36%)
Technical/Professional			2 (9.09%)	1 (4.55%)
Tertiary				
Not Available	2 (5.26%)			

Table 18
Medium of Instruction in Parents' Primary Education

Medium of Instruction	Fathers of Working Children (N = 38)	Mothers of Working Children (N = 38)	Fathers of Non-Working Children (N = 22)	Mothers of Non-Working Children (N = 22)
Chinese	36 (94.74%)	38 (100%)	18 (81.82%)	20 (90.90%)
Others	2 (5.26%)	0 (0%)	4 (18.18%)	2 (9.09%)

Educational background generally indicates a person's social status. However, in the Chinese community in Malaysia, a person may be lowly educated but it does not necessarily mean that he is poor. On the whole the Chinese are good businessmen. Lowly educated businessmen often acquire more wealth than educated Chinese. Besides, a person may be lowly educated, but if he acquires enough wealth, he may still enjoy high social status within the Chinese community. The writer suggests that some Chinese use all means to acquire wealth, including using child labour. This is indicated in the use of child labour as a strategy to maximise profit in some small-scale enterprises.

However, the low educational background of the child workers' parents explains their attitudes towards their children's educational need. As we shall see in a later section, many of them were of the opinion that if their children did not do well in school, they should leave school and work. To them although formal education is important, it is not considered essential for a person to survive or to be successful. They themselves had not got much education but they were able to make a decent living and they thought their children should be able to do likewise. The parents of non-working children who had better education could better appreciate the importance of formal education. Hence their concern with their children's schooling (see later section).

Parents' Occupation and Working Hours

Most parents of the working and non-working children in the sample were in employment, i.e. 68% of the parents of the working children as compared to only 54.54% of the parents of the non-working children were in employment.

Table 19 shows that both sets of parents were in similar occupations. Most of them were in business or engaged in manual work. Those who were in business were generally self-employed hawkers, shopkeepers (mostly coffee shops) and some were building contractors. Those engaged in manual work were generally lorry drivers or labourers in construction sites and in factories.

Table 19
Types of Jobs of Parents

Type of Jobs	Fathers of Working Children (N = 38)	Mothers of Working Children (N = 38)	Fathers of Non-Working Children (N = 22)	Mothers of Non-Working Children (N = 22)
Professional & Technical	5	1	2	1
Administration & Management	2	2	2	1
Clerical				1
Business	17	11	8	1
Manual Work	9	14	10	5
Agricultural	1	2		
Unemployed	2			
Housewife		8		9
Deceased	2			

A higher percentage of the parents of the working children were in business as compared to the parents of the non-working children. This tendency has two important implications. Firstly, as the volume of their business is rather large, many of these so-called "hawkers" were chicken suppliers for other businesses, such as eating stalls and restaurants and had very high income per month. Thus, some parents of working children might be wealthier than the parents of the non-working children. Secondly, as there is a higher possibility for children of self-employed parents to engage in work activities, their engagement in work activities may have nothing to do with poverty but rather is closely related with the nature of their parents' occupation as shall be discussed later in the next chapter.

Table 20 shows that majority of the working parents of the working children worked for much longer hours than the working parents of the non-working children.

Table 20
Number of Hours Parents Work per Day

Number of Hours	Fathers of Working Children (N=38)	Fathers of Non-Working Children (N=22)	Mothers of Working Children (N=38)	Mothers of Non-Working Children (N=22)
< 8 Hours	2 (5.26%)	1 (4.55%)	11 (28.94%)	5 (22.73%)
8 Hours	12 (31.58%)	12 (54.55%)	6 (15.79%)	6 (27.27%)
8-10 Hours	7 (18.42%)	3 (13.63%)	6 (15.79%)	1 (4.55%)
>10 Hours	12 (31.58%)	5 (22.73%)	6 (15.79%)	1 (4.55%)
Not Available	5 (13.16%)	1 (4.55%)	9 (23.68%)	9 (40.91%)

Table 20 shows that 50% of the fathers and 31.58% of the mothers of the working children worked for more than 8 hours a day. A high proportion of them worked for more than 10 hours a day. In comparison, only 36.36% of the fathers and 9.9% of the mothers of the non-working children worked for more than 8 hours a day. A higher number of mothers of the working children were also in employment and this means in many families where children worked parents had very little time for their children.

The difference between the number of hours parents of working and non-working children work is to some extent influenced by their occupations. Many parents of working children were self-employed businessmen while many parents of the non-working children were employed by others. However, the difference between number of hours parents of working and non-working children work, and the difference between the number of mothers of working and non-working children work indicate the relative economic strength of their families. The parents of the working children had to work harder to acquire enough income. This in a way indicates that the families of the working children were relatively poorer.

In two families where children work the parents were not staying with the children. In the first family the parents were separated and the three boys were left in the care of the grandmother. The parents only came to see their children once in a while. The boys joined a gangster group and dropped out of school. In the other family, the father was working in the United States of America as an illegal worker, while the mother worked in Klang. The children, comprising a girl and two boys, were left with their grandmother, who was in her 70s. The mother only came home to see her children once a month. The eldest daughter dropped out of school when she was 16 years old after her boyfriend (16 years old) made her pregnant. She went to work as a clerk in a factory.

The two cases show that children's participation in economic activities may have no connection with the economic situation of their family; instead it may be a result of bad parenting. The amount of time parents spent with their children is important to the children's socialisation. If parents do not spend enough time with their children the chances of their children becoming delinquent, drop out of school and end up in employment is higher.

Family Income

Family income is defined as income of both parents. In general, the Chinese are very sensitive when they are asked about their income and they will normally give a lower amount. The writer discovered this in many instances when interviewing parents of working children. Many of those who said their monthly income were between RM1,000 and RM2,000 might have given only their main income and excluded their side incomes. When the writer asked his informants to comment on the income level stated by these parents, they had the same opinion. If both parents were in employment as in the majority of the cases and their income was between RM1,000 and RM2,000, then on average they earned between RM500 to RM1000 each. Such income level was low considering child workers too could earn between RM500 to RM1,000 a month. Judging from their age (many of them were not old) and occupation (they have similar occupation as their children, in fact some of their children work for them) their income level must be much higher. Besides, as mentioned in Chapter 1, the majority of families in Balakong New Village owned houses and lands, which could be very valuable. Therefore, the writer believes only a few families of the working children were poor.

In Malaysia poverty is often measured by referring to the poverty line. The poverty line for 1997 is not available, however according to the Seventh Malaysia Plan the poverty income line in 1995 was RM425 per month for a household size of 4.6 in Peninsular Malaysia (1995:69-99). At the same time the incidence of poverty among Malaysians was only 8.9% in 1995, the incidence of poverty in urban area was merely 3.7% (1995:66-99). Given only the rough estimates of their parental income it is difficult to determine the percentage of child workers that come from poor families. However, bearing in mind that most of them came from small households, only the minority of them came from poor families when measured against the poverty income line. (See Table 21)

Table 21
Family Income

Income Level	Working Children (N=38)		Non-Working Children (N=22)	
Below RM500	1	(2.63%)		
RM500-RM999	5	(13.16%)	2	(9.09%)
RM1,000-RM1,499	9	(23.68%)	7	(31.82%)
RM1,500-RM1,999	12	(31.58%)	4	(18.18%)
RM2,000 and above	9	(23.68%)	9	(40.91%)
Not Available	2	(5.26%)		

Table 21 shows that the majority of these families earn more than RM1,000 per month. Some in fact earned more than RM2,000 per month. Only one working child's family income was below RM500. However, this may not be the real income level. The father worked as a lorry driver, the mother was a housewife. There were five children in the family and only one worked part-time. Therefore, this income level was low to sustain a family, but they did not seem to be in hardship. Only 15.79% of the working children's family earned less than RM1,000 per month. On the contrary, some working children's families appeared to be very rich. One working child's father admitted that he earned more than RM10,000 per month as a chicken merchant (hawker). Another family owned one of the two restaurants in the village, and business was very good.

However, Table 21 indicates that the families of non-working children were slightly better off economically than the families of working children. It must be stressed however that the income level shown in Table 21 may be an underestimate.

On the other hand, we cannot see any correlation between child work and family income. The distribution of working children among the family income categories does not show any relationship between the two variables. The mode family income is at family income between RM1,500 to RM1999. This shows that family income is not a significant factor that determines child work in Balakong New Village. In other words, it is a norm in Balakong New Village for children to work for some reason regardless of their family income.

A Synthesis

Generally, the demographic and family characteristics of child workers in Balakong New Village do not indicate that poverty is an important cause of child labour in Balakong New Village. Instead, some of the demographic and family backgrounds of the child workers, such as their parents' education, occupation and working hours, indicate that children's participation in work activities may be influenced by other factors.

In comparison the child workers' families had slightly lower income than the families of the non-working children. This is indicated in their family size and family income. However, this is not enough to conclude that child labour in Balakong New Village is caused by poverty. To show that child labour is caused by poverty one must show that child labour is an economic necessity, without which it will be difficult for the family to survive. In this study none of both the child workers and their parents said that the children worked out of necessity. Instead, they gave some other reasons why the children worked. When the parents were asked, what did they do with the money given to them by their children, only 7 parents said they used them as household fund. However, two of them added that they did not need the money, but since it was given to them they might as well use it. Other parents said they saved the money given to them by their children for their children. Besides, as it was discussed in Chapter 2, many child workers including full-time child workers continued to ask their parents for money. This shows that child work was not an economic necessity for the families concerned.

However in some cases such as in families that operate petty trading such as eating stalls, where the work involved is simple but time-consuming, it would not be profitable for the traders to hire people to work for them. To relieve some of their workload they often asked their children to help. In these cases it is somehow necessary for children to work to maximise the profit of their parents' business. Therefore, to some extent children in such families worked out of economic necessity. But this kind of economic necessity is not caused by poverty but is caused by the desire on the part of the family to maximise profit.

Nevertheless, it may be necessary to point out that since the child workers' families had lower income, it may be fair to say that relative poverty is a cause of child labour. However, the writer will try to show that relative poverty is but one insignificant factor among a set of interrelated social and cultural factors that cause a child to work. The writer believes that this is a valid interpretation of the finding because of the fact that there were poor families that did not send their children to work and there were rich families that asked their children to work. Besides, relative poverty alone does not seem to be able to force children to work. Often a combination of factors is necessary to make children work.

5

Social and Cultural Factors as Determinant of Child Labour

IN THIS CHAPTER THE WRITER tries to show the importance of social and cultural factors in explaining the existence of child labour in Balakong New Village. The social and cultural factors that will be discussed include parental attitudes and expectations towards child rearing and education, education system, juvenile delinquency, children's own value system, mode of production and the external environment of Balakong New Village. However, before examining the importance of these social and cultural factors, the writer will first examine the importance of poverty as a determinant of child labour in Balakong New Village.

Social and Cultural Factors

The discussion above shows that poverty is not an important determinant of child work in Balakong New Village. On the other hand, the writer believes a set of interrelated social and cultural factors are the more significant determinants of child work. The social factors include educational problems, juvenile delinquency, mode of production and the physical and social environments of Balakong New Village. Meanwhile, the cultural factors consist of children's value system, parental attitudes toward child work, education and child rearing.

Although many of these factors are discussed individually, it is important to point out that they are often interrelated to form a complex whole. Sometimes one factor is enough to make some children participate in work activities. At another time, a combination of a few factors is needed. At yet other times one or more factors may be able to prevent a child from participating in work activities.

Problems in Education and Juvenile Delinquency

Educational problems and juvenile delinquency are discussed together because the interplay between these two factors creates a complex phenomenon. Perhaps it is easier to begin with the academic performance of the children in Balakong New Village. Generally most of the full-time child workers in Balakong New Village were once weak students in school. The non-working children were better not only in their academic performance but also in their behaviour. This strongly suggests that a child's academic performance is somehow related to the child's behaviour. Eighteen (85.71%) out of the 21 parents of school dropouts interviewed said their children went to work because they were poor in their studies or they did not want to stay in school anymore. The writer believes there were two factors that caused the poor academic performance of these children, i.e. poor linguistic ability and delinquent behaviour. The poor academic performance of the children was caused by either one of these factors or both.

Balakong New Village is a Hakka dialect speaking community. The people here converse in Hakka in their daily encounters. The writer was told by key informants to try to speak the Hakka dialect when interviewing the villagers. They will be less co-operative as they feel distanced if the writer speaks to them in Mandarin. This extensive use of their mother tongue causes many children to be very poor in Bahasa Malaysia, English as well as Mandarin.

Most of the children in Balakong New Village attended the Chinese medium primary school in the village. According to a teacher who taught in the school for 15 years, although the enrolment rate was good, about half of the students were weak in their curriculum. They were especially weak in languages, including Mandarin. The school had conducted many programmes to help them but they were not very effective. According to the teacher there was no learning atmosphere in the village.

The weak foundation of students in Balakong primary school, especially their difficulties in mastering Bahasa Malaysia made it very difficult for them to follow lessons in the secondary school where the medium of instruction is Bahasa Malaysia. The one-year Remove Class did not seem to be effective in preparing them for lessons in Bahasa Malaysia at the secondary level. The difficulty in understanding the lessons in school made many of them lose interest in schoolwork. Thus they often skipped classes and switched their interest to something else. This in turn made their performance at school even worse.

The relationship between poor academic performance and delinquent behaviour is dialectical. One of the reasons why some parents thought that there was no point in keeping their children in school was related to absenteeism. Some parents claimed that they objected to their children's suggestion to stop schooling. A few parents said they had objected to the suggestion a few times but when their children kept running away from school, they were forced to give in to their children's decision because they simply could not constantly keep an eye on their children. An interview with the Senior Assistant of Cheras Perdana Secondary School,[5] which most students from Balakong Village attended, revealed that absenteeism was a very serious problem among students from Balakong New Village. The extent of the problem was not clear, as the writer was not allowed to see the school record.[6]

Normally, students from Balakong New Village go to school by school bus. The journey from Balakong New Village to Cheras Perdana takes about 15 minutes. As the school is at a distance from their home they can run away from school without the knowledge of their parents and other villagers. Furthermore, Cheras Perdana is on the way to Kajang. Many of them pretend to go to school but when they get off the bus in Cheras Perdana they do not go to school directly but proceed instead to shopping centres in Kajang. After a certain period of time when these students continue to skip classes and the school authority had tried their best to discipline them, the school authority has no choice but to suspend or expel some of them from school.

On one occasion in Balakong New Village a student was absent from school for about one year without his parents' knowledge. His parents only discovered this when the school

---

5 25 November 1997.

6 The Deputy Minister of Education, Dr Fong Chan Onn, said in 1994, about 1% of the students were absent from school throughout the year (*Nanyang Siang Pau*, 30 November 1995).

authority sent a teacher to see them. This is not surprising as many parents of the child workers, as mentioned earlier, had very little time for their children. The Senior Assistant continued to say that the school once organised a dialogue session with the parents in Balakong New Village on the discipline and academic performance of students from the village. Only a small group of parents of good students came to attend the dialogue.

The writer suspects some of the students may be absent from school to take up what they considered well paid jobs, as what happened in Penang. A group of students in the northern town in Peninsular Malaysia was reported to have skipped classes to work in golf clubs, retail outlets and workshops where they earned as much as RM25 per day (*New Straits Times*, 30 January 1996).

Absenteeism is but one among the many delinquent behaviours of the full-time child workers in Balakong New Village. Another problem is their association with gangster groups. There were two rival gangs in Balakong New Village, the *Hong Household* and the *Wah Kees*.[7] Normally those who joined the gangster groups were also the weak students, including a few non-working children. It seems that this is a way for them to identify themselves and distinguish themselves from others. This process can be regarded as a form of self-labelling, i.e. to indicate that they are a class of their own. The gangster groups give them an identity, which they could not find in school. This is probably the reason why only students with good academic performance join the Association of Secondary School Students.

---

[7] For a general description of the role of the secret societies in Chinese community please refer to Laurence K.L. Siaw, *Chinese Society in Rural Malaysia*. Kuala Lumpur: Oxford University Press, 1983.

To join the Hong Household the boys need not pay any entrance fee. However, they need to pay a monthly "protection fee" of RM5. To join the *Wah Kees*, the larger and stronger gangster group, the boys have to pay an entrance fee of RM18 and a monthly protection fee of RM5. In most of the fights among these boys the *Wah Kees* usually win. The *Wah Kees* boys were more delinquent and more aggressive than the Hong Household boys. The *Wah Kees* boys also had more activities.

Gangsterism in school as was found in Balakong is a widespread problem in Malaysia. The Ministry of Education had declared a very strong stand against it and encouraged school authorities to take stern action against students involved in gang activities (*Utusan Melayu*, 26 June 1995).

Although concrete evidence is not available, the writer believes some of the *Wah Kees* boys took soft drugs. One mother of the boys told the writer that she also believed her son took ecstasy pills. Smoking is very common among the boys as well as among the girls who mixed around with them. The boys' relationship with girls can also be promiscuous, as there were cases of pre-marital teenage pregnancy in the village.[8]

---

[8] The writer had witnessed a short episode when interviewing the *Wah Kees* boys one Saturday midnight after they came back from a disco. A group of about ten consisting of boys and girls were gathered in a video game centre managed by one of the boys. They were drinking beer. The girls were wearing makeup and dressed fancifully (or rather sexily). After interviewing about four of them, one of the girls seemed to be very upset about something. Shortly, the girls went out to have a discussion. In the conversation among themselves the writer discovered that there was a dispute between two girls. One of them went for a ride on the motorcycle of the boyfriend of another. This aroused some jealousy. The interview had to stop. A few days later the writer heard from Sian, one of the *Wah Kees* boys that the couple had broken up.

Mr Gan, the writer's key informant said when he was young and a member of a gangster group, some of his gang members were involved in group-sexual-activities, where one girl allowed more than one boy to have sexual intercourse with her at a time. There is no evidence of this practice among the teens under study. However, there were at least two out-of-wedlock teenage pregnancy cases during the period when the writer conducted fieldwork in Balakong New Village.

Fighting and gambling are two most popular activities among the boys The Senior Assistant of Cheras Perdana Secondary School told the writer that many students from Balakong New Village fought on the school bus during the journey to and from school. He denied any gangster activities in his school. However, he did not deny the involvement of his students in gangster activities outside the school compound. He also denied that there were racial fights, but one of the writer's key informants who also joined a gangster group said they sometimes fought with Malay boys.

During the period when the writer conducted fieldwork in Balakong New Village there was one fight between the Hong Household boys and the *Wah Kees* boys in the village. The fight took place in front of a video game centre. One of the Hong Household boys sustained a light injury on his head. The fight was initiated by an unfriendly gesture, i.e. staring at one another. This type of fight is very common among the boy gangsters. One of the child workers who brought the fight to the writer's attention also showed the writer a deep scar on his leg, which he claimed was sustained in a fight.

Gambling is common not only among teenagers but also among adults. Gambling activities could be witnessed easily in coffee shops and house compounds. One popular gambling activity in Balakong New Village was betting on horseracing and jackpot machines in the video game centres. There were around 10 video game centres in the vicinity of Balakong New Village, four in the village itself. Almost every video game centre had one of these two kinds of machine. The writer noticed that they were very popular. Besides gambling on the machines they also engaged in traditional gambling activities, i.e. playing cards and *majong*[9]. Pinn, one of the boy gangsters, said the amount of money spent in one gambling activity could ran up to several hundred ringgit.

Besides gambling many teenagers in this village also spent money on motorcycle and went to places like Karaoke bars and discos. Most of the time the boys would have to spend the girls who accompanying them. Some of them went to work because they wanted to buy their own motorcycle, if their parents did not buy one for them.

All these activities have at least three implications on child labour. Firstly, many of the boys and girls are expelled from school. One boy was expelled from school a few weeks before the writer interviewed him for being involved in a fight in school. Another boy was expelled from school for an overall poor performance in discipline.[10] One girl was expelled from school after running away with friends to Johor Bahru, Johor,

---

9 *Majong* is a form of traditional Chinese gambling method. There must be three or four persons to play this game. A set of tiles, normally made of plastic, with different symbols is used.

10 He was attending a Chinese vernacular school in Kajang. In this vernacular school students have to pass a certain grade for discipline to proceed with their study.

for some time. A few girls in Balakong New Village ran away from home. Another girl was stopped from schooling because she was pregnant. As mentioned above, the Minister of Education, Datuk Seri Najib Tun Razak, had given all Principals of schools the power to take stern action, including expulsion and suspension, against students with disciplinary problems (*Utusan Melayu*, 26 June 1995).

Secondly, their somewhat expensive lifestyles simply do not permit them to stay in school anymore. The boy who was suspended from school because of the fight was later given a choice to return to school, but he declined the offer. According to Pinn it was because he wanted to work to pay up his gambling debts, which run up to several hundred ringgit. Many of the full-time child workers said their salary was not enough to pay their expenses, therefore, they still asked money from their parents. Thirdly, these boys are not interested to stay in school as the institution imposes so many restrictions on them. Surely, their academic performance would not be good if they were not interested in their studies. Besides, the school authority would be happy to let them drop out, as their performance will affect the overall performance of the school.

As shall be explained later, for the majority of the parents if their children are not doing well or not interested in school, it will be better for them to get a job, which they did. Therefore, it is clear that educational problems, juvenile delinquency and child labour are inter-related.

Mode of Production

Rodgers and Standing (1981a:13) define mode of production as "a specific set of social relations of production and distribution combined with a related development of the forces of production". In its macro sense we normally look at the stage of Industrial development of the society. Malaysia as a whole and Balakong in particular is in a transition from an agrarian to an industrial society. Many plantations had been transformed into industrial areas. As Malaysia is still a developing country, factories in Malaysia are mostly small and medium size and labour intensive. Hence the factories need to employ a large number of cheap foreign workers to be competitive. Besides using foreign workers the writer believes these factories also use child workers to make the industry competitive. On the other hand, as job opportunities in these factories are plentiful many children are happy to leave school when they do not do well in their studies.

How parents or close relatives' productive activities are organised (Schildkrout, 1981:99), is useful in explaining some of the cases of child work in Balakong New Village. Here the works of some part-time family child workers were clearly related to their parents or relatives' productive activities.

As discussed earlier in this chapter, the nature of the hawking business is such that it would not be profitable for the hawker to hire people to work for them because the work involved is simple and routine. It would be a waste to employ outsiders and pay them wages for that kind of work. Furthermore, during the past 10 years the economy of Malaysia was so good that not many people would like to work for a hawker stall for low wages. Therefore, many of these hawkers would have to take their children or relative's children to work for them and pay them a small stipend or none at all. The writer notes many of the hawkers in Balakong now hire foreign workers, mostly Bangladeshis, to work for them. Hence, it is believed that if not for these foreign workers more children will be working in this sector.

The concept of family enterprise that is important to the Chinese also contributes to the existence of child labour. Every member of the family is expected to help the main breadwinner, after all they benefited from the business and have a prospect of inheriting it. Besides, this is also a way for the children to show their *xiao* (filial piety). Two fathers expressed this perception in very clear terms. The first said according to Chinese tradition, 'children are expected to help their parents in their parents' work (family enterprise) so that the parents' work can be lightened.' The second agreed and added that he 'thinks every Chinese parent would expect the same'. This is a common expectation among Chinese parents, although the writer discovered that there were parents in Balakong New Village who thought differently.

In the cottage industry, when one member of the family contracted the work to be done at home, other family members, including children would join in to do the work. It becomes a kind of family activity. As explained in Chapter 2 they worked while watching television and talking to each other. They could work as and when they like. Therefore, many of them did not perceive this as work proper, but a kind of game to fill their free time and to bring them some small income. Besides, many children felt good to help a family member to finish a job contract.

It is clear that the nature of part-time family work is very different from part-time non-family work. The meaning of work for children who worked for their parents in hawker stalls is different from the work done by children engaged in hawker stalls owned by unrelated person. The former is part and parcel of the children's family obligation, while the latter is only a means to make some money.

Children's Own Value System

In many studies child workers are portrayed as pitiful victims of some family misfortune. However, as we have seen in the previous section, in Balakong New Village children themselves play an important role in determining whether they work or not. As illustrated earlier the lifestyles adopted by some boys makes it difficult for various reasons for them to remain as students. In fact, 15.19% of the child workers interviewed said they took the initiative to work and to look for jobs. On the other hand, 42.86% of the full-time child workers interviewed said they like working more than schooling, while 33.33% were not sure. However, 66.67% of the full-time child workers said they had no intention to go back to school. Many of those who said they like to work said they were motivated by money.

It would be much more telling if we look at the cases of the part-time non-family child workers. The majority of part-time workers in non-family enterprises are opportunists, who take advantage of any available opportunity to make some easy money. Many of them frankly told the writer that they worked for the money[11], although they might not like the job. Here we can see clearly how the emphasis on material wealth in the Chinese culture influences the practice of child labour.

Some part-time family child workers were not asked by their parents or relatives to work. Normally these children worked for reasons of their own. For example, one boy likes to

[11] See Chapter 2 on how they spent their wages.

work in his uncle's coffee shop because when he goes out to work, he gets more freedom, as his uncle does not control him as much as his parents. During his free time he can play in the video game centre near his uncle's coffee shop, where he can also meet some of his friends.

Peer influence is also an important factor. Many of these child workers, whether they worked full-time or part-time, play and work together. The girls who served beer are a typical example. A few of the girls said they did not like the job, but since their friends were going to work they simply followed. About 23% of the children interviewed said they knew of the job opportunities or got the jobs through friends.

These children are therefore not "forced" to work, but opt to work on their own initiative.

Parental Attitudes

Parental attitudes are important determinants of child work. Parental attitudes can directly or indirectly determine whether children participate in economic activities or prevent them from doing so altogether.

1. Attitude on Child Work

More than 50% of the parents of working children disagreed with the proposition that children have a right not to work (see Table 22). Among them 10.53% strongly disagreed with the proposition. Only one parent of the non-working children disagreed with the proposition. More than 50% of them agreed with the proposition, while the rest were neutral about it.

When these parents were asked to explain their position, the writer discovered that they did not understand the proposition in terms of abstract rights and duties. Instead, they considered the proposition in relation to children's education.

Table 22
Positions of Parents on the Proposition that Children have Right Not to Work

Position	Parents of Working Children (N = 38)	Parents of Non-Working Children (N = 22)
Strongly Agree	0.00%	0.00%
Agree	26.32%	54.55%
Neutral	7.89%	40.91%
Disagree	50.00%	4.55%
Strongly Disagree	10.53%	0.00%
Not Available	5.26%	0.00%

Many parents of the full-time child workers viewed child work as an alternative to schooling. They were very concerned with what their children would do if they were not allowed to work after they dropped out of school. They thought it would be good for those children who dropped out of school to learn a skill by having a job. Besides, work will also keep these children occupied and keep them away from vice activities. Some parents of both full-time and part-time child workers also believed work is important to train children to be diligent.

On the other hand, the parents of the non-working children were very concerned about their children's education. They did not want their children to work because they believed it would affect their children's academic performance. Although they also wanted their children to be diligent but they wanted them to be diligent in their study first. Some of the parents of the non-working children also expressed concern about the safety of children at work. This is an issue that very few parents of the working children raised. The writer believes they were aware of the issue because of a few cases of work accidents involving children in Balakong New Village. However, they take this as a fact of life that should be tolerated and accepted.

It seems that there is a clear correlation between the attitudes of parents towards child work and the incidents of child work. However, it is possible that the attitudes of the parents of the working children were affected by the academic performance of their children. Had their children performed well they might change their attitudes and discourage their children to work. The core issue here appears to be the children's education.

2. Parental Attitudes on Education

Generally, the parents of the non-working children had higher and clearer expectation of their children's education. Table 23 shows that a higher percentage (40.9%) of the parents of the non-working children wish their children to receive tertiary education. However, only 18.42% of the parents of working children have such a desire. A higher expectation in their children's education makes the parents of the non-working children more concerned with their children's education. One of the results of this concern is that they do not allow their children to work, fearing that this may affect their children's academic performance.

Table 23
Parental Expectation in Education

Parental Expectation	Parents of Working Children (N = 38)	Parents of Non-Working Children (N = 22)
Tertiary	18.42%	40.91%
Secondary	7.89%	22.73%
Primary	0.00%	0.00%
As High as Possible	52.63%	27.27%
No Expectation	15.79%	9.09%
Not Available	7.89%	0.00%

Besides having a higher expectation the parents of the non-working children also had a clearer expectation. While the majority of working children's parents said they only expected their children to receive as much education as possible or had no expectation at all, the parents of the non-working children normally stated clearly what they expected. Some of them might not have high expectation but they at least had a minimum expectation, such as their children should at least pass Form Five. The writer believes this clearer expectation help both the parents of the non-working children and the children themselves to have a direction or a target to achieve. On the other hand, the parents of working children allow circumstances to decide their children's fate, and lack the drive to overcome their children's problems such as linguistic problems at school. Therefore these children are more likely to be poor students and leave school early.

However, some parents of the working children who have a higher expectation of their children's education view child work as a form of training. As alluded to earlier, they believe work make their children more skilled, practical and more diligent. In addition some of them think it would be good for their children to learn to do business early, thus encourage their children to help them in their business.

3. Parental Attitude on Children's Moral Development and Success

Generally, parents of both working and non-working children were unable to state clearly what moral virtues they wished to inculcate in their children, apart from saying that they wished their children to "behave well". However, most of them promptly agreed that *xiao*, diligence and honesty are important virtues to be inculcated in their children.

While the parents of working children are more inclined to view material achievement as a symbol of success, parents of non-working children regard being knowledgeable as an important symbol of success. Hence they have higher expectation in their children's education.

The parents of the non-working children are more concerned with their children's moral development. Many of them made an effort to see that their children did not turn delinquent. For example, some bought computers for their children to play computer games at home to prevent them from going to the video game centres. Others made efforts to know their children's friends. In particular, some of them were very concerned with the effect of work on children's behaviour. They noted that many children became more delinquent after they began working. This is also one of the reasons why some of them did not allow their children to work. Generally, as alluded to in Chapter 2, they tend to spend more time with their children.

Besides discovering how parental attitudes determine, directly or indirectly, whether children work or not, we can also see how the traditional Chinese cultural values, such as the emphasis on *xiao*, diligence, material wealth and education, influence the practice of child labour, although sometimes the relationship may not be clear. The parents of working children and non-working children differ as to which of these values is given higher priority.

External Environment

The term "Environment" here is taken in both the physical and social sense. Physical environment here refers to the existence of certain facilities, such as factories and video game centres. On the other hand, social environment concerns public opinion about child work. Although the external environment is only an indirect determinant of child work, it is nevertheless very important, as it often provides a conducive environment for the other factors to take effect.

As indicated in Chapter 1, Balakong is a developing Industrial area. There are seven industrial parks within 10km in the vicinity of Balakong New Village. Several hundreds of factories are operating in these industrial parks. As discussed above, these are mostly labour-intensive small and medium size factories. This has created a high demand for factory workers. A casual survey conducted in these industrial parks indicates that many factories are looking for workers, as evidenced by banners hung outside their factories. A casual conversation with a committee member of the Association of Landowners and Factory Entrepreneurs (Pesatuan Pemilik Tanah dan Pengusaha Kilang) of Balakong Industrial Area, also revealed that there is a shortage of manpower. This is probably the reason why some factories take in child workers or contract out work.

Some employers of child workers were approached for an interview. Only two co-operated. The first employer was the owner of a bus assembly factory that employed a few child workers. However, he talked only about his nephew whom he thought was a little too young (15 years old) to work full-time. However, since his nephew was not interested in studying anymore, work might be an alternative for him. Besides, if his nephew worked for him, he could watch over him, so that he would not get into bad company, although he was never seen with the boy gangs. He was aware that employing children in factory is illegal, he believed the enforcement authority would not take stern action. Another employer was a vegetable seller who employed a 16-year-old boy. The boy had worked for her since he was 13 years old. Initially, the boy worked part-time. However after he dropped out of school he began working full-time. She said she did not want the boy to leave school and was saddened to see the boy left and became delinquent, as she treated him like her own relative. She said she employed child workers mainly because no adult would want to work for a vegetable seller.

The video game centres in the vicinity of the village seem to be responsible for the delinquent behaviour of many children. It is common gathering spot for many of these child workers at night. Many parents of both working and non-working children complained about the number of video game centres operating in Balakong New Village, as there are more than ten video game centres in the vicinity. Recreational facilities for healthy activities, such as sports are obviously lacking in the village. The only healthy recreational activity available is playing basketball in the primary school basketball court. Adults normally occupy the only football field in the village.

Although parents, community leaders, political leaders and the villagers are aware of the problems caused by video game centres, and that most of the video game centres operate without proper licensing, nothing much was done about them. According to the State Assemblyman and a few community leaders, there are three groups of people: the local video game centre operators, the gangsters and the police, who have an interest in the running of these video game centres. It is difficult for them to do anything against such a strong combination of people.[12] The involvement of the locals, the gangsters and the police are obvious. The writer personally witnessed a group of police entering a video game centre without taking any action against both the video game centre management and those under-age teenagers who were playing inside. The police should have taken action against the owner of the video game centre for operating the centre without proper licensing and allowing minors (below 18 years old) to enter the centre.

---

[12] The state government is very concerned with this problem. However, the district offices dare not take strong action, according to the State Assemblyman of Balakong. However, the district office's worry is understandable, as the State Exco Official, Datuk Fuad Hassan, himself was threatened by the gangsters for taking tough action against the video game centres (*Star*, 18 November 1997).

In short, there are ample opportunities for vice, while there is an obvious shortage of facilities for healthy recreational activities.

The majority of political and community leaders, as well as villagers interviewed were of the opinion that children below 16 should not work. However, they did not condemn child labour. Instead, they were more concerned with the effect of work on the education of children, as they said children should concentrate on their schoolwork rather that working. Nevertheless, some of them made exemptions for children from poor families and low achievers at school.

Although many villagers disagreed with child work, only a few were ready to do something when a case of illegal child work came to their knowledge. Most of them kept their opinions to themselves. The same was true with local political and community leaders. Although they do not agree with child work, they do not think that this issue should be given high priority in their agenda. What occupied the highest priority in their agenda were basic problems such as floods, poor garbage collection and the poor road condition, which the villagers were most concerned with. A check on the minutes of meeting of the village's Committee for Development and Security (Jawatankuasa Kemajuan dan Keselamatan Kampung), which is responsible for the affairs of the village, revealed that the problem of both child labour and juvenile delinquency were never discussed. Nevertheless, the Association of Secondary School Students was initiated by the local MCA branch to organise activities such as seminars and tuition classes to motivate the children in Balakong New Village. But these activities failed to attract the delinquent teenagers. Nevertheless, it does become a forum for the good students to have some healthy activities. In short, there is a lack of public opinion against child labour in the village.

Conclusion

The practice of child labour among the Chinese in Balakong New Village appears to be influenced by some social and cultural factors. Child labour seems to be a by-product or consequence of the some other social problems. While in some cases a single factor is enough to make children participate in work activities, in others the interplay of a set of social and cultural factors cause child labour.

Full-time child labour is mainly a consequence of the failure of the education system in dealing with weak and delinquent students. When the system fails to keep the child in school, work seems to be the nature result. On the other hand, the interplay between some social factors and parents or children's attitudes results in children working part-time.

Therefore, child labour should not be viewed as merely a result of economic misfortune but as a complex socio-cultural phenomenon.

6

The Impact of Child Work

Introduction

IT IS OFTEN CLAIMED THAT children participating in economic activities are exposed to serious risk on their physical, emotional and moral health. In almost all the previous studies conducted in Malaysia only negative impact were highlighted. The absence of positive impact in these studies is meant to show that child labour should reasonably be condemned. In the writer's judgement although these studies have shown that child labour is to some extent harmful, however, the severity of the harm caused by child labour shown in these studies may not give enough moral ground to condemn a culturally approved practice. In this chapter the writer will examine the impact of work on the children in Balakong New Village, to show whether this negative impression of child labour is justified. The writer will go further to show that child labour, in some circumstances may either be beneficial or necessary.

Physical Health

As explained in Chapter 2 many children, especially those who work in factories, small workshops and construction sites, were engaged in "hazardous work". The major concern with child labour is due to its negative impact on children's physical health. This is implied in the overriding concept "hazardous work", which is defined as "work that is likely to jeopardise the health, safety or moral of children" by convention No.138 of the International Labour Organisation. Although moral wellbeing of children is mentioned in the definition, the physical health of children is often the focus of attention.

The biological characteristics of children are different from adult because they are still in the process of growth and development. This difference in biological characteristic according to Forastieri (1997:10) makes children more susceptible to work hazards. The writer provides a comprehensive list of work hazards, which children at work are exposed to, i.e. occupational accidents, occupational diseases and ergonomic hazards (1997:8-29).

Some training may be needed for children to use some of tools and equipment. Besides, great care must be taken when they use these tools and equipment. Children are normally relatively less well trained to handle these tools and equipment. They are also less conscious about safety at work. These make occupational accidents more prone among child workers as compared to adult workers. Furthermore, the tools and equipment children used at work and the work methods are normally designed for adult. Therefore, the special need of children is normally not taken into consideration when these work methods, tools and equipment were designed. Therefore children using these work methods, tools and equipment run a higher risk of fatigue and injury. Children at work are also exposed to harmful agents, such as heat, noise and dust. Due to their special biological characteristics children are more likely to acquire occupational diseases.

Although this study shows that many child workers were exposed to work hazards, not many children were seriously injured during work. Half of the full-time child workers said that they were once injured during work. However, in most cases the kind of injuries they sustained were minor wounds, i.e. cuts that needed no professional medical treatment. However, in few cases these children needed a few stitches. Among the part-time child workers only some sustained minor injuries, such as cuts and burns once during work. These part-time child workers were working in eating stalls and the cottage industry.

However, there were few cases of serious work accidents involving child workers from Balakong New Village. For example, a sawing machine cut off portions of two fingers on the right hand of a boy who worked in a furniture factory when he tried to cut a piece of wood. He was hospitalised for two days. However, he left the hospital and did not follow the full course of medical treatment. This worsened his condition, and now he is unable to stretch his fingers. For this injury, he only received RM2,000 as compensation from his employer. His family did not take any legal action against his employer because they felt bad to do so against someone they know well. Besides, they were also worried that if they took action against the employer no other employer would want to hire the boy. This incident shows civil law may not be able to protect the interest of child workers.

One of the key informants, a former child worker, also had a portion of his middle finger on his right hand cut off by a sawing machine during work. Later, when he was helping his parents to tap rubber the same finger was clamped by a machine used in rubber production causing a fracture. In another incident, a metal cutting machine also cut off a small portion of this middle finger, when he worked in an engineering factory. For all these injuries he received no compensation.

Another boy who worked for a company which has businesses in many Southeast Asian countries was luckier. He fell from a rooftop as he was installing a ventilation system on the roof, and sustained a seriously broken arm and was hospitalised for two weeks. He had to be laid off for one whole year. However, his employer paid him about RM6,000 as compensation, plus all the medical expenses incurred during hospitalisation and the following check-ups for one year. After that he went back to work in the same company. He and his family were very happy with the arrangement and had no intention to sue his employer.

Besides the immediate impact of child work on the child, its impact on children's physical development too need to be studied and evaluated. However, as the writer is not medically trained, it is beyond the writer's ability to do so, except to make some superficial observations. For example, the writer observed that a relatively tall boy who worked for his father in a small motorcycle repair workshop used to squat and bend his back and legs while working on motorcycles for many hours a day. This has caused him to be slightly hunchbacked.

However, it seems that the work hazards that affect child workers are partly due to the nature of the work and partly due to mishandling of tools and machinery, carelessness, as well as ignorance of children's development. Therefore, it is believed that the situation can be improved if employers, parents and child workers are educated about these matters.

Education

We have seen in the previous chapter that many parents, community leaders and villagers who disagreed with child work were worried about its effect on children's education. We have also seen that child labour in Balakong New Village is closely related with children's poor academic performance. Many of those who were expelled from school went to work because they needed an alternative to schooling. While those who left school on their own free will normally saw no more future in schooling and felt that it was better for them to work. Therefore, to some extent child work is both the result of leaving school and the reason for leaving school.

In this section the writer tries to explain the interrelationship between child work and education. Although there is no strong evidence, but there are indications that part-time child work affect children's academic performance. A close examination of the result of Year-end Final Examination, in the year before and after the part-time child workers in Balakong Primary School began working revealed that 50% of them had declined more than 10% in their academic performance after working. The writer also discovered that some of these children only worked as little as one hour per day. Perhaps works made them lose concentration in their schoolwork, as they have less time. Besides, 54.17% of all the child workers in the primary school were already low achievers. Therefore, there was not much room for further decline in performance. So, child work is very likely to have affected the academic performance of these child workers. Besides, it is very likely that many of these child workers will end up dropping out of school when they are promoted to secondary school, as it will be more difficult for them to cope with the school work, if they do not do something to improve themselves now. This is possible because a number of the full-time child workers began working when they were still in school. In short, for many of these child workers, time should be spent on their schoolwork instead of working, if they want to do better academically.

It is important to point out that child work does not seem to affect many children's interest in schooling. Only 2 (3.38%) out of the 53 part-time child workers said they like working more than schooling, while 12 (22.64%) were not sure of their position. Out of these 14 part-time child workers, only one did not want to stay in school, while 6 were not sure.

Many child workers (including full-time child workers) who did not want to continue schooling were affected by their own assessment of their academic ability. Many of them believed that they were not good academically and saw no hope of getting through the third year secondary examination, the PMR (Penilaian Menengah Rendah) or SRP (Sijil Rendah Pelajaran Malaysia). It is clear that this examination had discouraged them to continue schooling.

Many parents, as stated earlier, see child work as an alternative to schooling as it enables children to acquire some useful skills. However, the effectiveness of this alternative depends very much on two factors, i.e. the willingness of employers/ masters to impart skills and the duration the child will stay in one occupation. Many child workers indicated that their employers/ masters were rather keen to impart skills. This is evidenced in the child workers' ability to perform skilful jobs such as welding, handling machinery, repairing motorcycle and installing car accessories, as explained in Chapter 3. If we bear in mind that these children were delinquent juveniles and low achievers in school, their ability to perform these skills is impressive. But as we have seen in Chapter 3, many child workers changed their occupation rather frequently, mainly because they were not very sure of the type of career path to take. This could affect the effectiveness of child work as a form of skill training. This will also have adverse effects on the child workers' career prospects, as shall be explained later.

Work experience also enables good students to learn some useful skills and to bear responsibilities. This is supposed to contribute positively to their socialisation processes. Work makes many of these children more practical as they were dealing with concrete situations in business and the working world, rather than abstract knowledge in books. Besides, certain abstract subjects they learned in school such as mathematics can be put to practical use at work. For example, those who help in hawking were often receiving and changing money, which allowed them to use mathematics in a concrete situation.

On the other hand, children were sometimes entrusted with important tasks such as taking orders and minding stalls or workshops when their parents or employers were not around. Bearing responsibility can make a child more mature.

Emotional Health

It is often reported that child workers are fatalistic. This is only natural if these children are victims of family misfortune. However, this did not seem to be the case for majority of the child workers in Balakong New Village. When these children were asked whether they were happy working and with their jobs most children were unable to distinguish between the two concepts clearly. Therefore, the answers they gave which were here taken to be the answer to both questions. It was found that the majority of them (68.35%) answered the question affirmatively. The main reason for this is obvious; most of them were not forced to work by family misfortune.

There were generally three main reasons why they were happy with their work/job. Firstly, many of these children were satisfied with their income. This is not surprising as we have seen in Chapter 3 that at their age many of them were rather well paid, and their pay enabled them to pursue many of their interests freely. Secondly, many of them, especially the full-time child workers said although they worked for long hours, they were not pressurised at work. This should be understood in relation to the pressure in school. Most of these child workers were once poor or uninterested students who faced loads of schoolwork and examinations in school. Besides, some of their employers were rather lenient with them. Some of these child workers indicated that their employers treated them like friends. Thirdly, many child workers felt that what they learned in their work are something practical, something that they could use to make a living. In contrast, schoolwork is abstract and irrelevant in their life. In one extreme case, by working as a motorcycle mechanic the boy achieved his ambition. This shows that these children had limited ambition, all they wanted is to make a living. It is perhaps others like the writer who impose on them ideas that they never think of. Some part-time child workers see their work as a kind of enjoyable activity that brings in income. Therefore they do not see work as a burden.

However, some of these children might not be honest about their feelings because some expressed their regrets in leaving school and that they would like to go back to school if they were given another opportunity. However, some took positive steps to deal with their regrets, such as taking English lessons, perhaps in preparation for future learning in private institutions.

Over 17% of the child workers said they were unhappy with their job. The majority of them were part-time family child workers. This indicates again that the general explanation is valid, as most of the part-time family child workers were asked to work. Since they were more likely to be unwilling to work, they were more likely to be unhappy. Nevertheless, they gave a variety of reasons for their unhappiness as stated out below:

1. They had to do too much overtime work.
2. Their work was very tiring and tough.
3. They faced a complex work environment and nasty people during work.
4. They were afraid of making mistakes as they might be scolded.
5. They learned nothing at work.
6. They did not like dirty environment.
7. They felt restricted.

Reasons 1 and 2 above show that a few children might be overloaded with work. This is not only detrimental to their physical health but also detrimental to their emotional health. Reasons 3 and 4 indicate that children might be prematurely introduced to a harsh work environment. This was especially true among the girls who serve beer. One of the girls told the writer that on one occasion she was surrounded by a group of drunken men, who asked her to drink with them. This is something no decent people want a 16-year-old girl to face. Reason 5 shows that sometimes work may not be an effective alternative to schooling. Reason 6 indicates that some child workers were working in unsatisfactory environment. Some sites where children work, such as factory and kitchen are poorly maintained, and it is clearly not suitable for children to work in such environment. While as any kind of work need a certain degree of discipline, this may disturb the emotion of children who are naturally playful. This, however, can be good for them, as some form of discipline is needed in children's socialisation process.

The rest of the child workers (13.92%) were not sure whether they were happy with their jobs. Many of them, especially full-time child workers, were aimless. Two boys expressed this aimlessness clearly. One of them said: "What to do? If I am not going to school, I have to work". "Whatever job is the same, at least for now", said another boy. Some of them started working presently, so they still have no idea what they wanted. Perhaps, it depends on whether the money is good or not.

Moral Health

In the Chinese culture idleness is seen as a source of all sorts of vices. Therefore, many parents believe that if their children are not schooling they should be working. Working, as opposed to idleness will prevent children from becoming delinquent. One father expressed this perception very clearly when he said that by allowing his son to work he was sending his son to be "educated" (disciplined) by others, since he had failed to do so properly. To some extent this perception is accurate, provided children are working in good environment. One needs some discipline in work, and the employers will also make sure that his employees have some discipline so that their jobs will be well done.

However, in the first place we must distinguish the impact of dropping out of school from the impact of working. The writer believes that once a delinquent child drops out of school it is very likely that he will become more delinquent. This is because dropping out of school means he has more time to pursue other activities including vice. Besides, without the control of the school authority means he also has more freedom to do what he likes. Whether work helps to instil some discipline in him depends on the work environment.

However, in most cases the parents' objectives are not attained, as their children do not become better after they start working. Instead there is a possibility that they become more delinquent. In their work environment children are often exposed to various bad influences and have more opportunities to pursue activities society deems to be only suitable for adults, such as drinking. As they work among adults, they may pick up some of these activities from their adult colleagues.

On the other hand, having their own source of income will give them more autonomy. Many of the activities the child workers pursue, such as gambling and going to discotheques are expensive. Before they begin working they had to rely on their pocket money to pursue these activities. Now that they have their own source of income they can pursue such activities more freely. There is evidence to show that child workers pursue such activities more actively when they get their pay. Some child workers told the writer that they normally would go to karaoke bars or discotheques to celebrate when they received their monthly salary. There was also an incident where a child worker lost about RM200 on the horseracing machine immediately after he received his salary.

Materialism is probably another moral danger that child workers face when they have access cash. As it was discussed above many children were happy with work because of the money they earned. We have seen in Chapter 3 that many child workers spent most of their salary on things like entertainment and expensive clothes. Many part-time child workers worked for this reason. When their pay is inadequate to purchase clothes and for entertainment, such as in the case of factory workers, many girls can easily be persuaded into prostitution.

In short, if properly managed, child work may be beneficial to children's moral development because to some extent it imposes some discipline on children and allows them to bear some work responsibility. But, if child workers are exposed to various forms of vice in their work environment, child work could be very detrimental to children's moral development. Unfortunately the writer observed that in Balakong New Village only very few full-time child workers were not delinquent.

Long Term Impact

In the previous sections the short-term or immediate impact of child work were examined. However, the magnitude of some of the impact of child work could not be examined except over a long period of time. One such impact is the career prospect of child workers.[13]

---

13 This is closely related to the claim that child work is an alternative to schooling.

In this section we will examine a sample of life/work history of former child workers, who are now in their twenties or thirties. They were asked to look back into their lives and work history and state whether they were happy with it.

The case studies show that if a child worker acquire enough skills and capital, it will not be difficult for him to move up the social hierarchy, from a skilled labourer to a small time businessman. As indicated in Chapter 1, this is a common pattern of social movement in the 19th century Southeast Asian Chinese community. However, capital is essential for the skilled labour to move up the social hierarchy.

Frequent change of occupation led the child workers nowhere, as they had not acquired enough skills in a particular job to become skilled workers. This to some extent reduces their earning ability. These examples show that child work can be an alternative to schooling if it is carefully planned. However, in the majority of cases, the child workers do not plan their career. In most cases they need many years of work experience and often try a few jobs before they know what they want in life.

However, in all cases lack of schooling had brought some setbacks to the former child workers. All of them are wiser now and would like to receive more education if they are given another opportunity. Some children may not like schooling, but a few years later, many of them would regret leaving school early.

Conclusion

It seems that child work is to some extent detrimental to children. However, we should not overlook its positive impact and its function as an alternative to schooling, when other alternatives are not available. Perhaps, the harmfulness of child work depends very much on what children are exposed to in work, how they work and how their working lives are planned.

7

Child Labour Law

Introduction

IN THIS CHAPTER, THE WRITER wishes to critically examine the Children and Young Persons Act 1966, the present law that regulate child work in Malaysia. Some of the international instruments, which propose to regulate child labour, will also be considered, to see whether they can be adopted in Malaysia. It is hoped that a better law can be proposed in the light of this study.

There are a number of relevant international instruments on child labour. They include the United Nations Declaration on the Rights of the Child (1959), the Convention on the Rights of the Child (1989), the World Declaration on the Survival, Protection and Development of Children (1990) and the International Labour Organisation's Minimum Age Convention 1973 (No.138). While all these international instruments mention the rights of children against child labour, more emphasis will be given to the Minimum Age Convention 1973 as it is a measure specifically designed to deal with the problem of child labour. In Malaysia, the law that regulate child work is mainly found in the

Children and Young Persons (Employment) Act 1966. As we shall see, the provisions of this Act are similar to that of the international instruments, except that the provisions of this Act are much more lenient than the international instruments. It is said that the more lenient provisions are to take into consideration local cultural values. (Yaqin, 1996:160)

Outline of International Instruments

Generally, most of the international instruments aim to impose a duty on the member states to prohibit child labour. What makes the International Labour Organisation's Minimum Age Convention 1973 different from the rest is that it does not only declare the rights of children, but also aims to abolish child labour in the long run, and to protect children at work in the short term, by providing specific measures. In addition to that it also takes a flexible approach, allowing its member states to progress through stages.

Normally not all kinds of child labour are prohibited by these international instruments. Only child work that would affect the health, education, or interfere with physical, mental and moral development of children are prohibited. A good example is in the United Nations Declaration on the Rights of the Child (1959). Besides its concern with the general welfare of children, Principle 9 also states that:

> "The child shall not be admitted to employment before an appropriate minimum age; he shall in no case be caused or permitted to engage in any occupation or employment, which would prejudice his health or education, or interfere with his physical, mental or moral development."

United Nations Instruments

Besides the United Nations Declaration on the Rights of the Child there are a few other United Nation's instruments that have some bearing on child labour. The following list of relevant instruments are produced by Fyfe and Jankanish (1997:82-83):

— **UN Convention on the Rights of the Child** (entry into force: 2 September 1990; 187 ratifications as at 31 January 1996), see especially Article 12 and 13 (freedom of expression and right of children to express views on their life); Article 15 (freedom of association); Article 19 (protection of children from injury, abuse, exploitation, etc.); Article 27 (adequate standard of living); Article 28 (right to education including free compulsory primary education); Article 32 (protection from economic exploitation) and Article 34 (protection from sexual exploitation).

— **International Covenant on Economic, Social and Cultural Rights** (entry into force: 3 January 1976; 133 ratifications); see especially Article 10(3) on child labour; 11(1), 12(2)(a), 13(2)(a) (compulsory education) and 14 (progressive implementation of compulsory schooling).

— **International Covenant on Civil and Political Rights** (entry into force: 23 March 1976, 132 ratifications); see especially Article 8 (prohibition on slavery, servitude, compulsory labour) and 24 (protection of minors).

— **Supplementary Convention on the Abolition of Slavery, the Slave Trade, and Institutions and Practices similar to Slavery** (entry into force: 30 April 1957; 114 ratifications); see especially Article 1(d) referring to debt bondage of children.

- **Convention for the suppression of the Traffic in Person and of the Exploitation of the Prostitution of Others** (entry into force: 25 July 1951; 70 ratifications). This instrument refers to earlier instruments that are still in force for many countries, including the **International Convention of 30 September 1921 for the Suppression of the Traffic in Women and Children**, as amended in 1947 (in force for 42 countries).

Of all these instruments, the United Nations Convention on the Rights of the Child 1989 is the most relevant instrument to child labour. This convention will become binding on the state once it is ratified by the state. Although Article 32 of the Convention refers specifically to economic exploitation, however exploiting child worker could result in violating many other Articles of the convention. In Fyfe and Jankanish's (1997:84) opinion, there is good opportunity to develop national programmes and policies against child labour around the central principle of the "best interest of the child", i.e. the central principle of the convention, since virtually all countries have now ratified the convention.

International Labour Organisation Instruments

The International Labour Organisation has declared abolition of child labour as one of its main objectives since its establishment in 1919. However, the Organisation does not oppose all types of child work. For example the Organisation does not oppose child work that is an integral part of the socialisation process of children, which allows parents to transmit skills to their children. Instead the Organisation is concerned with situations where children are compelled by poverty to work on a regular basis to earn a living for themselves or their families. It is believed that these children are often forced to do work that affect their physical, mental and social development (Bequele, 1986:14).

The International Labour Organisation's convictions on child labour are as follows (Fyfe and Jankanish, 1997:76):

a) Childhood is a period of life, which should be dedicated not to work but to education and development;
b) Child labour, by its nature or because of the condition in which it is undertaken, often jeopardises children's possibilities of becoming productive adults, able to take place in the community;
c) Child labour is not inevitable and progressing towards its reduction and even its elimination is possible when the political will to fight it exists.

In this study we see that these convictions may to some extent be in conflict with the Chinese culture in Malaysia. Although the Chinese will agree that education and development are important to children, they sometimes consider child labour as an alternative to or a form of education to make children productive adults. In some circumstances the Chinese also consider child labour an inevitable fact of life as not all children do well under our education system. If this belief is proven true than the Organisation should allow these types of child labour to continue as long as the child workers are carefully protected. As discussed above the Organisation does not oppose child work that is an integral part of children's socialisation process. However, the Organisation does give flexibility in Convention No.138 for member states, whose education system are not so well developed to provide a more lenient law, as shall be discussed in more detail.

To achieve the Organisation's objective the Minimum Age (Industry) Convention 1919 (No.5) was adopted immediately after the Organisation was formed, to prohibit children less than 14 years of age to work in industrial undertaking. Since then the Organisation had also adopted a series of conventions fixing the minimum age of admission to employment in different sectors, these sectors include employment at sea, agriculture, trimmers and stokers, non-industrial employment, fishing, and underground work.[14] Convention No.138 is a consolidation of these earlier conventions. It is applicable to all sectors of the economy. In the preamble to the Convention, it is stated that: "the time has come to establish a general instrument on the subject, which would gradually replace the existing ones applicable to limited economic sector, with a view to achieving the total abolition of child labour". However, this does not mean that the earlier conventions are no longer valid. If a country is still not ready to commit to a general instrument, it can ratify the earlier conventions on a specific sector of the economy (Swepston, 1986:22).

In the long run Convention No.138 aims to abolish child labour by fixing a minimum age under Article 2 for children to enter into employment or work (regardless whether children are paid or not). The minimum age shall be the age when children finish their compulsory education and in no case shall it be less than 15 years. The ratifying state shall progressively raise

---

[14] For details of the development, see Bouhdiba, *Exploitation of Child Labour*. New York: United Nations, 1982:28-33.

this minimum age to a level where the physical and mental development of children are at its fullest. However, the Minimum Age Recommendation, 1973 (No.146) recommends 16 years as the minimum age. In the case of hazardous work Convention No.138 sets the minimum age at 18 years. However, if the health, safety and morals of children are fully protected and adequate instruction and training are provided, children may engage in work that is considered hazardous at 16 years of age. The lowering of minimum age for hazardous work is a flexible approach of Convention No.138. Convention No.138 also allows progressive implementation of the convention. For ratifying states that have insufficiently developed economy and education system the general minimum age may be set at 14 years. On the other hand, Article 7 provides that a member state may allow children aged between 13 years and 15 years to be employed to do light work, which is unlikely to affect children's health and development and education. As for those countries, which have specified 14 years as the basic minimum age for children to be employed, the minimum age for light work can be further reduced to 12 years.

Besides allowing member states to lower the minimum age, the convention also allows member states to limit its application to limited categories of employment or work and limited branches of economic activity. Article 4 of the convention provides the member states with a wide discretion to exclude categories of employment or work from the application of the convention, if enforcement of the convention in the categories of employment or work is not feasible. However, the member state must first consult the appropriate employers' and workers' organisations and there must be special and substantial problems of application before a particular category of employment or work can be excluded. However employment or work, which is likely to jeopardise the health, safety or moral of children, cannot be excluded. Work in family undertaking, followed by domestic work is most frequently excluded from the application of the convention (Swepston, 1986:23). To further limit abuses of the discretion, Article 4 also requires the member state who wishes to limit the application of the convention to list the categories of employment or work excluded in the first report to the International Labour Organisation, and states the reasons for such exclusions. The member state that wishes to limit the application of the convention must also state the position of the law and practice in respect of the categories of employment or work excluded in its subsequent reports.

Article 5 of the convention also allows member states whose economy and administration facilities are insufficiently developed to apply the convention to limited economic sectors. However, the general condition of the child worker in the excluded sectors must be reported regularly, and the following seven sectors must be covered:

> "Mining and quarrying; manufacturing; construction; electricity; gas and water; sanitary services; transportation, storage and communication; and plantations and other agricultural undertakings (excluding family and small-scale holdings mainly producing for local consumption and not regularly employing hired workers)."
> — (International Labour Organisation, 1996:26)

Article 5 is a measure to encourage those countries whose economy and administrative facilities that are insufficiently developed to adopt convention No.138, instead of earlier conventions, as convention No.138 is intended to slowly replace the earlier conventions.

However, the International Labour Organisation recognised that setting a general minimum age for children to engage in any type of work can only be achieved in the long term. In the short run it has adopted some measures to protect children against exploitation by prohibiting certain types of work and regulating others.[15] Recommendation No.146 suggests that measures should be taken to protect children or young person under the age of 18. Paragraph 13 recommends that there must be provision on:

a) Fair pay, in accordance with the principle of equal pay for equal work;
b) Strict limitation on hours spent at work in a day and a week. Overtime work should also be prohibited. This is to ensure enough time for education, training, play and leisure;
c) A minimum of consecutive of 12 hours' night rest, and customary weekly rest days;
d) Annual holiday with pay of at least four weeks or not shorter than that given to adults;
e) Social security scheme;
f) Standard of safety and health, instruction and supervision.

---

15 For details of the measures, see ibid.

Malaysia has taken this position, i.e. to protect children at work from exploitation. However, the labour standard set in the present law is much lower than that recommended by Recommendation No.146.

Apart from Convention No.123, Minimum Age (Underground Work) 1965 and Convention No.29, Forced Labour 1930, Malaysia has not ratified any International Labour Organisation Convention on child labour.

Child labour was placed on the agenda of the 86th Session (1998) of the International Labour Conference (International Labour Organisation, 1998:1). New instruments were proposed to deal especially with the intolerable or extreme forms of child labour, as the problem of child labour in the world is still serious (International Labour Organisation, 1998:9). The proposed instruments differ from the other instruments in that it focuses entirely on extreme forms of child labour, and there are no exceptions on coverage irrespective of the country's level of development. This is because the instrument is supposed to deal with intolerable forms of child labour (International Labour Organisation, 1998:10). Malaysia is one of the many countries that agree to this new instrument. However, Malaysia is of the opinion that the new convention need not apply to all children under the age of 18 years, consistent with other international instruments. Instead, Malaysia is of the opinion that the minimum age should be specified in national law on the condition that health, safety and morals of children are fully protected (International Labour Organisation, 1998:39). This indicates that Malaysia's commitment to the new instrument is not strong.

The proposed definition of "extreme forms of child labour", which Malaysia agrees, is as follows (International Labour Organisation, 1998:42-43):

a) All forms of slavery or practices similar to slavery, sale and trafficking of children, forced or compulsory labour including debt bondage and serfdom;
b) The use, engagement or offering of a child for prostitution, production of pornography or pornographic performances, production of or trafficking in drugs or other illegal activities;
c) The use or engagement of children in any type of work which, by its nature or the circumstances in which it is carried out, is likely to jeopardise their health, safety and morals.

Outline of the Malaysian Law

In Malaysia child labour is regulated by the Children and Young Persons (Employment) Act 1966. This section will outline some of the important provisions of the Act. Generally, this Act does not strictly prohibit child labour, in the sense that child participation in many kinds of work activities is permitted by the Act.

Basically, the Act aims to regulate, as opposed to prohibit child work. However, the standard of protection is much lower than the standard proposed by the International Labour Organisation. Yaqin (1996:160) comments that the law seems to be founded on the assumption that child labour is acceptable to local culture, therefore strict prohibition will not be effective or even detrimental. This is especially evidenced in Section 2(2)(a), where "employment involving light work suitable to [a child's] capacity" is specially permitted within family undertaking. This could be due to the fact, as this study shows, that it is very common in our society for children to participate in family undertaking. However, in the writer's opinion, as we shall see in more detail, this Act does not respond to the local culture successfully.

General Prohibition of Child Labour

Section 2(1) of the Act provides that both children and young persons are prohibited from engaging in any "employment", except those permitted by the Act. It must be noted that the subsection only prohibits "employment" and not "work". In other words the Act only prohibits "wage employment". Section 1A(1) of the Act defines "employ" and "employment" to mean "employment in any labour exercised by way of a trade or for the purpose of gain, whether the gain be to a child, young person or to any other person"; and "employer" to mean "any person who has entered into a contract of service to employ any child or young person and includes the agent, manager or factor of such first mention person." Therefore, parents or relatives who ask their own children or a relative's child to work for them are not employers, unless there is a formal contract of service or employment. A contract of service or employment is needed for the Act to apply. The Act will also not apply in situations where children or young persons are working as independent contractors (for example in the cottage industry). Therefore, both children and young persons can engage in any "work" activity, under any condition, as long as they are not "employed". The prohibition is very narrow even if no exception is provided. However, as there are also many exceptions to the prohibition provided by the Act, the scope of protection offered by the Act is very narrow. However, this weakness does not exist in Convention No.138, as it is intended to be applicable "to all sectors of economic activities, whether or not the children are employed for wages" (International Labour Organisation, 1996:24). The term "employment" in Convention No.138 means any form of work regardless of the formal employment status of children (International Labour Organisation, 1986:22).

The Exceptions to the General Prohibition

The Act defines those who have not completed 14 years of age as children, while those who are older than 14 years but have not completed 16 years of age, as a young person. The exceptions to the general prohibition in the case of children and young persons differ. Therefore the writer will treat them separately, although there is some overlap between the provisions.

1. **Provisions for Children:**

   Generally, children are permitted to engage in four categories of "employment" provided under section 2(2):

   a) Employment in a family undertaking to do light work;
   b) Employment in public entertainment, licensed under this Act;
   c) Employment as part of a training programme approved or sponsored by the government;
   d) Employment as an apprentice under an approved apprenticeship.

These provisions appear to be reasonable. However, these provisions are ambiguous. For example the term, "light work" is difficult to define (K.S. Jomo, et al., 1992). This study also shows that the conditions of children engaged in family work may be poor. So ideally, the law should provide some protection to children against unscrupulous parents or relatives.

Further conditions for employment are provided in Section 4 and Section 5(1). Section 4 provides that no children or young person shall be allowed to work continuously for more than 6 days in seven consecutive days. This is obviously a very low standard, as it is usual for most adults to work for only 5½ days in a week and 6 working days in a week is only a minimum standard provided by the Employment Act 1955 to protect adult workers. It seems that the law allows children or young persons to work for longer hours than a normal adult worker.

Under Section 5(1) children are not allowed to work under the following conditions:

a) Between 8pm to 7am;
b) Continuously for more than three hours without at least thirty minutes rest;
c) More than six hours a day, or the sum of schooling time and working time cannot be more than seven hours;
d) To begin a day's work before a fourteen hours' rest.

It should be pointed out that these conditions are in line with the International Labour Organisation's Recommendation No.146, clause 13. However, some recommendations of the Recommendation No.146, such as those relating to pay and fringe benefits, are not accepted fully. On such issues, children and young persons are treated by the Act as equivalent to adults, as provided by the Employment Act 1955.

Section 5(2) excludes children employed in public entertainment from the restriction under Section 5(1)(a). This provision seems to suggest that the law will give way when the nature of work requires it.

2. Provisions for Young Person:

Young Persons are allowed to engage in the following employment under Section 2(3):

a) Employment that children are allowed to engage in and is suitable to his capacity, whether or not in a family undertaking;
b) Employment as a domestic servant;
c) Employment in any office, shop (including hotels, bars, restaurants and stalls), godown, factory, workshop, store, boarding house, theatre, cinema, club or association;
d) Employment in industrial undertaking suitable to a young person's capacity;
e) Employment on any vessel under the personal charge of his parent or guardian.

These provisions are so broad that they cover almost all kinds of employment. Such a wide provision makes the general prohibition of little meaning. Although section 2(3)(a) and (d) specified that the work must be suitable to the capacity of a young person, there is no clear definition as to what is meant by " suitable to the capacity of a young person". It is also not clear, for example under Section 2(3)(d) whether young persons are allowed to work only in certain kinds of industrial undertaking, where its method of production is deemed suitable to the capacity of young person to participate in it, or young persons are allowed to work in any kind of industrial undertaking, as long as they only do work that are suitable to their capacity. If the interpretation is the latter, then this will make the law extremely difficult to enforce, as the inspector does not only need to prove that the young person is working in an industrial undertaking, he also has to prove that in that industrial undertaking the young person is doing work that is not suitable to his capacity. The requirement of the suitability of the work to the capacity of a young person is not provided under section 2(3)(b), (c) and (e). Therefore, it is also not clear whether young persons who work in these places or perform these types of jobs must also do work that is suitable to their capacity.

Despite the above provisions the Minister responsible for labour may allow a child or a young person to be engaged in an employment not mentioned as an exception, with or without imposing conditions, if he is satisfied that it is not hazardous under Section 2(4). This section suggests that children and young persons are allowed to engage in work that is not mentioned as an exception, as long as they get the approval of the Minister. This provision makes the exceptions to the general prohibition even wider. Nevertheless, the Minister may prohibit a child or a young person from participating in any detrimental employment under Section 3.

However, under Section 2(3) a female young person is not allowed to work in hotels, bars, restaurants, boarding houses or clubs that are not managed or controlled by her parents or guardian. Nevertheless, with the approval of the Director General female young person can work in a club not managed or controlled by her parent or guardian.

Section 4 also prohibits young persons from working continuously for more than six days. Here young persons are treated like adults under the Employment Act 1955. Under Section 6(1) young persons are not allowed to work under the following conditions:

a) Between 8pm to 7am;
b) More than four hours without a thirty minutes rest;
c) More than six hours a day or the sum of schooling time and working time cannot be more than seven hours;
d) To begin work before a fourteen hours' rest.

However, Section 6(2) provides that (a) shall not apply to young person employed in agricultural undertaking, public entertainment or in any vessel. These exemptions are against the general objective of the Act. Therefore, it seems that the spirit of the Act is that young person should be protected from bad working conditions as long as bad working conditions is not an inherent nature of his work. However, when the inherent nature of his work requires him/her to work under bad conditions the Act will provide an exemption, such as in the case of agricultural undertaking, public entertainment or in a vessel where sometimes require a person to work between 8pm to 7am.

Additional Provisions

The Act further provides in Section 2(5) that no child or young person can be employed contrary to the Factories and Machinery Act 1967 and the Electricity Act 1949. Under the Factories and Machinery Act 1967, a young person, who is a person who has not completed his sixteenth year of age, is not allowed to manage, attend or work in proximity to a machinery. While the Electricity Act 1949 (Revised 1973) prohibits a person below sixteen years, to be employed to manage, attend or be in proximity to a "live" apparatus not effectively insulated.

Section 7(1) of the Children and Young Persons (Employment) Act 1966 provides that a person may not employ a child or young person in public entertainment, unless he acquires a licence from the Director General of Labour or from his authorised representative. The Director General may prescribe some conditions in the licence. The Director General will not grant a licence if he is of the opinion that the employment will be dangerous to the life, limb, health or morals of the child or young person. [Section 7(2)]

Section 8 empowers the Director General to prescribe a minimum wage for any class of work, after inquiry into the nature or the conditions of the class of work. However, this power has never been exercised.

Enforcement Mechanism

The Department of Labour, under the leadership of the Director General of Labour is responsible for the enforcement of the Act.

The Act is enforced by way of inspections. Every year the Department of Labour has to undertake about thirty thousand inspections. One can imagine the number of inspectors needed and the cost involved in carrying out these inspections. As a result, the Department of Labour only inspects establishments that are registered with them. And, there are about 198,000 places of employment registered with the department in 1993 (Abdul Rahim, 1993:17).

Under Section 14, upon conviction the offender will receive a fine not exceeding RM2,000 or imprisonment for a term not exceeding six months, or both. In the case of subsequent offence the maximum fine is increased to three thousand and the maximum term of imprisonment is extended to two years (Section 14). The government proposed to increase the fine to ten thousand and make it compulsory for employers to register child workers, but to date these have yet to materialise (*Star*, 6 December 1995).

Effectiveness of the Law

Perhaps, the fairest way to assess the law is to see whether it achieves its stated purpose. In this case the Children and Young Persons (Employment) Act 1966 seeks to protect children and young persons against exploitation and detrimental work conditions. We have seen in earlier sections that there are obvious inherent weaknesses in the law itself and the labour standard demanded by the law is low. However, if we take the labour standard as it stands, there are still numerous violations of the low standard. This shows that working children are barely protected.

Take the full-time child workers in Balakong New Village for example. The law states that children and young persons are not allowed to do work that involve management of, or attendance on, or proximity to, any machinery and live apparatus not effectively insulated. However, as it is found in this study there were so many children working as machine operators in factories and as assistant electricians. Children and young persons were also engaged in work like welding and work that involve climbing to a high place. Although these are not works that involve heavy load but it is questionable as to their suitability to the capacity of children and young persons.

With regard to working conditions, the law is also widely violated in the case of children in Balakong New Village. Among the respondents there were 8 (28.57%) full-time child workers who worked for more than 6 days in a week. All the full-time child workers worked for more than 7 hours in a day. This has not included overtime work. Some child workers were still working after 8pm in the evening. This is clearly in violation of Sections 5(1) and 6(1) of the Children and Young Persons (Employment) Act 1966.

Although most of the part-time child workers are engaged in works that are permissible by the law, most of their work conditions violate the condition specified by the law. Night work was very common, as they were going to school in the morning or afternoon. Most child workers who did night work were those who were engaged in hawking, serving beer and working in cottage industry. There were also three part-time child workers who were required to work for more than 6 days in a week. As children and young persons spend about 5 hours in school for their normal school day, children are only allowed to work for not more than 2 hours and young persons are allowed to work for more than 3 hours, in their normal school days. For the children and young persons are not attending school, or during school holidays or weekend, they are not allowed to work for more than 6 and 7 hours respectively. However, 33.33% of the part-time child workers worked longer than this time limit. The majority of part-time child workers, especially family workers, were not given a break in between their work hours as specified by Section 5(1) and 6(1) of the Children and Young Persons (Employment) Act 1996.

It seems that in many cases the use of child labour in Balakong New Village violates at least one of the conditions set by the Act. However, in many cases "employers" of these children had not committed an offence, as there was no employment contract between them and the children. Even in cases where employment contract exists the law was still not enforced. There were places where children work such as, at home, which is virtually enforcement free. The weakness of the present enforcement mechanism, by way of inspection of work place is very obvious. The ineffectiveness of the present enforcement mechanism is shown clearly in the fact that from 1986 to 1990, for example there were less that 10 convictions under the Act each year, while thousands of inspections had been conducted in a year (Abdul Rahim, 1993:18).

Besides, we must be careful that an ineffective child labour law such as the present Malaysian law may make the position of the child workers worse, instead of helping or protecting them. It is often argued that child labour law often pushes children to work in the informal sector that is difficult to regulate. This study discovers that many child workers are not given the fringe benefits prescribed by law due to the illegality of their employment. When there are accidents they may not be compensated and their families are reluctant to take legal action against their employers because they thought the children might have also committed an offence by being a child worker.

The writer believes that Bequele and Myers (1995:87) are not wrong to point out that law is an important instrument to protect children from work hazard or even eliminating child labour. However, as pointed out by Rodgers and Bullock (1972: 181) with regard to civil rights in the United States the "mere passing of a law and the development of machinery to institute and enforce that law does not guarantee that meaningful change will occur".

One important prerequisite of an effective law that regulates a practice that is approved by an established culture is that it must respond correctly to the established culture (Cotterrell, 1984:64; Podgorecki, 1974:253). The legislature must be able to use some elements in the culture to formulate the intended social idea and the law that enforces the idea. Thus, law becomes, in Bohannan's (1994:795) theory, a "double institutionalisation" of the existing culture.[16] The law should be able to achieve its intended ends, without offensively interfering in established culture.

There are clear examples of costly failures in the attempt to use law to alter established culture. The most well known example is perhaps the United States' attempt to prohibit the manufacture, transportation and sale of alcoholic liquor in the 1920s and early 1930s. Although more than 750,000 people

---

[16] The present writer is aware of the limitation of Bohannan's theory. However, the present writer finds his idea useful in solving the problem facing us.

were arrested and severe punishments were imposed, and more than $205,000,000 worth of property was seized, yet the law had very little effect on the alcohol consumption of Americans. The law was repealed as a result of massive protest, especially when "respectable citizens" were put in jail under the law (Cotterrell, 1984:59-60). In another example, the United States' Supreme Court tried to prohibit polygamy among the Mormons in 1896. The church leaders announced that God too had prohibited polygamy. Many Mormons were arrested for polygamy. Yet polygamy survives among the Mormons (朱景文, 1994:153).

The conflict between culture and law is especially apparent when a foreign law is received. The British experience in India is a very telling example. The colonial government tried to enforce the local culture, i.e. Hindu and Islamic law, in court, following common law procedure. The result was total chaos in the Indian legal system. Some anthropologists point out that culture is a living phenomenon. Once a cultural norm is enforced in court, it becomes static. Therefore it is manipulated (朱景文, 1994:154).

Therefore, the more successfully the law responds to the culture the less resistance the law will face and hence the more effective will the law be.

Child labour law in Malaysia did not grow out of the local culture. Rather it is a product of foreign influence, i.e. international pressure. Therefore, careful study of its compatibility with the local culture is necessary if it is to be effective in achieving its noble purpose of protecting the welfare of children.

Awareness and Effectiveness of the Law

The most effective law is one that is able to create a norm of obedience. Besides, the public's willingness to report cases of violation is also an important factor influencing the effectiveness of the law. In this study parents, who have a lot of control on whether children work, are obviously unwilling to obey the law. The villagers in Balakong New Village are also unwilling to report to the authority any violation of child labour law.

Awareness of the law and the impact of child work are important factors that influence the willingness of parents to obey the law and the public's willingness to report cases of violation. In this case the awareness of the Children and Young Persons (Employment) 1966 is very low. Only 53.13% of the villagers were aware of the existence of the law. However, none of them could state one of its rules accurately. The nearest answers were perhaps: "Those who are below 16 cannot work"; and "There is a limit to the working hours". The awareness of parents of working children were even lower, only 9 out of 38 (23.68%) parents said they were aware of the law. Again, none of them could state any of the rules accurately. The nearest answers were perhaps: "Those who are below 16 cannot work"; and "children are not allowed to do dangerous work". One possible reason for the low awareness of the law among parents of working children is that they want to use their "ignorance" to justify the fact that their children are working.[17]

On the other hand, 40.9% of the parents of non-working children said they were aware of the law. Nevertheless, when

---

[17] As there is a saying in Chinese that "no offence is committed by those who are not aware" (不知者不罪).

asked to state one of the rules, none of them gave an accurate answer. The answers that they gave are much the same as those given by parents of working children. Nevertheless, to a small extent we may conclude that parents' awareness of the law does influence the practice of child labour.

Obviously, there is a clear need to educate the public about the law. But, as Aubert (1966) stated in his study of the Norwegian Housemaid Law of 1948, that the influence of the law will depend on its ability to communicate a message to the housewives and housemaids without legally trained intermediaries. We may say the child labour law must be able to communicate a message to the parents, employers and general public without the help of lawyers. Generally, the present law is difficult to be communicated to the public, as the law is too detail and complex. Therefore, to be effective, we need a clear and simple law.

However, clearness and simplicity of the law alone is not a guarantee that the law will be effective. In this study parents of working children were given a hypothetical situation, where children who are 16 or below are clearly prohibited from participating in work activities. They were asked in this situation would they still allow or send their children to work? One third (33.33%) of the parents of full-time working children said they would still allow or send their children to work. Many of those who said they would still allow or send their children to work expressed their concern as to what should their children do if they are not going to school anymore. To them it is better to violate the law by sending their children to work than let their children stay idle and become lazy or more delinquent. While 47.62% said they would not allow or send their children to work. Almost all of these parents (except one) actually did not want their children to work. They wanted their children to stay in school and study more, however, as indicated in Chapter 4 they were unable to control their children. If the law clearly prohibited child labour, it may be a good opportunity for them to keep their children in school. The remaining 19.5% said they were not sure and the majority of them did not give their reasons.

On the other hand, 31.25% of the parents of the part-time working children said they would still allow or send their children to work. Generally, they did not think that prohibiting child labour was good for the children for various reasons. Interestingly, some of them distinguished work that was good for children, such as helping parents and some light work, from work which was dangerous. They said they would still send their children to do work that was beneficial to their children. While 56.25% of the parents said they would not allow or send their children to work. Many of them did not give their reasons but a few of them said they did not want to violate the law. The remaining 12.5% said they were not sure.

It seems that a clear prohibition of child labour will be more effective than the present law. However, there were still one third of the parents of the working children who were prepared to violate the law. It seems that parent's opinions about the law and child labour is another important determinant of the effectiveness of the law. We have seen in Chapter 4 that the majority of the parents of working children do not agree that their children have a right not to work. This is probably one of the reasons why they are willing to violate the law. Therefore, besides being clear, the law must also communicate a message that is acceptable to the subjects. The subjects must be convinced that the law is in their favour and not to create inconveniences to them. In other words, the subject must be able to internalise the value behind the law. Besides, the law must be able to deal with the social and cultural factors that influence the practice of child labour.

The present law assumes that poverty is the root of the problem of child labour; therefore, it tries to protect the children at work from exploitation and work hazards in the short term, and hopes that economic development will do the magic of eliminating child labour. It is submitted that this hope will be futile, at least in the Chinese community under study. The assumption simply misses the point all together. A simple prohibition of child labour or the setting of a minimum age for children to engage in work activities will be more effective than the present law. However, it will still leave some issues without answer and may cause some hardship to certain people. Take for example those who drop out of school. What should they do if they are below the minimum working age? In such a circumstance work seems to be a reasonable alternative to many people, including parents, although they do not agree to children dropping out of school and entering the job market at this young age.

8

Conclusion

Findings of the Studies

THE PRESENT STUDY AIMS:

1. to examine the influence of social and cultural factors on the practice of child labour, particularly in the Malaysian Chinese community;
2. to look into the conditions of child work and their impact on children participating in work activities because they are important for policymaking;
3. to find ways in which the law can respond to the social and cultural factors that influence the practice of child labour.

It is found that although Balakong New Village is a prosperous community, child labour is still rather widespread in this community. Children are found working in various sectors of the economy and are engaged in various types of job, either full-time or part-time basis. The rapid and ongoing development surrounding this community does not seem to eliminate child labour in this community, instead it has created numerous work opportunities for children. Children are found working in factories and small workshops shows that industrialisation will not eliminate child labour. Child workers who previously worked in the agricultural sector may have simply gone to work in the factories.

The full-time child workers are normally school dropouts whose natural option is to look for a job. These are the weaker students in school. They are normally boys from fourteen to sixteen years of age. The situation of part-time child workers is more varied. They can be boys or girls of as young as nine years old. The working conditions of the part-time child workers are also more varied as compared to the full-time child workers.

This study discovers that child workers normally come from families who are relatively poorer but who are by no means poor in the absolute sense. Their families may be "relatively" poor but this does not prove that poverty is the cause of the child labour for several reasons. First, it is difficult to explain why there are families with similar economic status do not send children to work. Second, this study shows that child work is not a necessity because the income of children is not needed for the families to survive. Third, most of the families of the child workers are not living in poverty as indicated by their demographic and family characteristics. Many child workers' families are well above the poverty line and most of the child workers spend their earning for themselves, on things like entertainment.

Some social and cultural factors may be better explanation of children's participation in work activities in Balakong New Village. Here we see the influence of the interplay between some social and cultural factors. Firstly, poor academic performance and juvenile delinquency are probably the main determinants of full-time child work because they cause children to drop out of school. Many children in Balakong New Village are weak in Bahasa Malaysia. This in turn affected their interest and confidence in other subjects, which are taught in Bahasa Malaysia, and consequently they drop out of school. Others are expelled or suspended from school for disciplinary problems. Many of the full-time child workers are involved in gang activities like fights, gambling, and probably drugs as well. Besides their expensive life style, for example they like to go to karaoke lounge and disco, does not allow them to stay as students. On the other hand, the Chinese culture put strong emphasis on diligence, therefore many parents expect their children to get a job if they are not going to school.

Secondly, the mode of production of the parents is the main reason of part-time family work. It is the nature of hawking business that it does not make good business sense to hire workers. For this reason many parents ask their children to help them in their work. In the cottage industry, work often becomes a kind of family activity. When one member of the family contracted work from a factory, other members of the family including children will work on it together. Helping parents or relatives is often seen by the Chinese as a way to express children's *Xiao* and diligence.

Thirdly, the children's own value system is also an important determinant of their participation in work activities. Very often, children are not asked to work, but volunteer to work. Many of them go to work because they know that there is an opportunity to earn some money. This is especially true of the part-time non-family child workers. Peer influence is another important factor for some children to participate in work activities. Children in Balakong New Village normally get their job through their friends, and often a group of them work together. The children's behaviour reflects the Chinese's value on material wealth.

Fourthly, parental attitudes towards children's work, education, moral development and future achievement can often decide whether children participate in work activities. There are not many parents who disagree with child work. Often working is seen as a good alternative to schooling, especially when children show no interest in schooling. On the other hand, participating in work activities is seen as a form of socialisation to make children more diligent and disciplined. Some parents even believe that children are obliged to help their parents in their parents' work. Parental expectation of children's achievement and level of education also have an important influence on whether children work or not. Normally, parents who have a higher or clearer expectation would not allow or send their children to work because they want their children to concentrate more on their studies and gain entrance to a university, as they see this as the first step to success. While the parents of the working children often take a more liberal position to let their children decide for themselves. It is more likely for the children of these liberal parents to perform poorer in school or to become delinquent and subsequently drop out of school while other children take this liberty to do some part-time work to earn some money. The influence of the Chinese value on diligence, *Xiao*, education and material wealth and the interplay among them and other social factors, are clearly the root cause of child labour in Balakong New Village. The difference between the parents of working and non-working children depends on which value the emphasis is.

Finally, the physical and social environments of Balakong New Village encourage the practice of child labour. Inadequate facilities for healthy activities make children turn to unhealthy activities like going to video game centres, karaoke lounge, disco, gambling and so on. These activities make children delinquent and drop out of school as a consequence. The industries surrounding the village have also created a great demand for child workers. The lack of unfavourable public opinion and governmental sanctions against child labour allow the practice to persist.

A more recent ILO report (Jensen, 2000) has begun to give more attention to social and cultural factors affecting child labour. It is stated in the report that:

> It is useful to begin with a framework regarding factors that affect child labour. There is of course no one cause of child labour, nor any one model adequately explain so complex a phenomenon. However, it is worth discussing in some detail the underlying theories behind why various factors are thought to affect child labour. Such an exploration makes it possible to coherently organise disparate observed facts and patterns, assertions, observations and questions about child labour and schooling.

Turning to the impact of child work on child workers, it is found that many children are working under conditions that are detrimental. Many of the child workers are required to work for long hours and for many days in a week. However, many of them are well paid for their hard work. Nevertheless, the work conditions of part-time child workers are normally better than the full-time child workers' work conditions. Besides, many of the full-time child workers are required to perform hazardous tasks as alluded to earlier. It must be pointed out that contrary to common belief, the family child workers, especially the full-time family child workers, are often required to perform hazardous tasks and worked under poorer conditions.

Physical injuries during work are not very frequent but when it happens it can be very serious. Child work has also affected the education of many child workers, though this may not be the case for all. For the good student, the work experience may be a good training ground. For the school dropouts, it is a reasonable alternative to schooling as they can learn some useful skill. But for the average students it is an added burden that they may not be able to cope with. However, the majority of the child workers are happy with working and their work. There are a few child workers who are not happy with their work or work environment, or are simply unhappy to work. Nevertheless, the most worrying impact of child work is that there seem to be a dialectical relationship between child labour and juvenile delinquency. Many children become more delinquent after they begin to work, although their parents are hoping that work will somehow instil some discipline in them. In the long run, lack of schooling may bring some setbacks in these child workers' lives; in particular it makes it hard for them to build their career. A few lucky child workers may be able to make a reasonable living but most of them live in low self-esteem for years. This is likely to happen to many full-time child workers in this study as in a very short span of their working lives, many child workers have at least changed their occupations once. This is especially bad for the full-time child workers as it hinders their opportunity to acquire enough skills in an occupation and subsequently affect their future career development.

The present Malaysian law that claims to protect children at work is not effective at all. Although the labour standard the Act sets is already very low compared to the standards set by international instruments, yet violation of the Act is still very widespread. The ineffectiveness of the present law can be due to a few reasons. Poor enforcement, inherent weaknesses of the law and lack of awareness are important reasons. However, the fundamental reason is that the law is unable to convince its subject that the law is necessary and beneficial. Social realities such as the weaknesses in our education system and juvenile delinquency induce many people to believe that child work is a natural alternative to schooling, even though they are aware that child work can be dangerous. On the other hand, child work is viewed as an important means to socialise children. It is seen as a means to make children more diligent and more filial.

Although the above observation is very important, without a thorough understanding of the various social and cultural factors affecting child labour, the effort to combat child labour will never be effective. As stressed by a recent ILO report (Jensen, 2000):

> In the community, cultural and societal attitudes towards children and work are important. It may be that children are afforded little value or rights. Or it may be that work for children is not viewed as undesirable. It may be that work is considered a part of socialisation into society for young children (especially boys), as in

> West Africa. In a context in which child labour is not shunned but perhaps even valued, efforts such as building schools may not have a great impact on reducing child labour unless information and attitudes are also addressed in an appropriate way. These issues also point out that the way to combat child labour will be both culture specific and must be culturally sensitive.

In conclusion this study shows that in Balakong New Village and possibly in other Malaysian Chinese community as well, poverty is actually not the most important cause of child labour. Instead, social and cultural factors are more important causes. Although child work may have some positive impact on children, the negative impact of child work should not be taken lightly. The ineffectiveness of the law is to a great extent due to the actual cause of child labour, i.e. social and cultural factors, which the law does not take into consideration.

Policy Implications of the Study

The extent of child labour, its impact on children and the ineffectiveness of the Children and Young Persons (Employment) Act 1966, strongly suggest the need to consider alternative approach to regulate the practice. Before we go into concrete recommendations, a few principles for effective child labour law that emerge from this study should be pointed out.

An over-generalised legal policy trying to control all forms of child labour under one policy should be avoided. We have seen in previous chapters that child labour can take many forms. Standing (1982: 614) puts it very interestingly that:

> One factor impending that is a tendency to over-generalise. Thus, sweeping moralistic denunciation of all forms of child work risk being manipulated by apologists to retain child labour as a means of accumulation or as a means of preserving a set of social relations of production. So the first principle of those wishing to assess State policies critically is to distinguish between forms of child activity that should be subjected to de-mystification, exposed as exploitative and oppressive, and those that are, if not acceptable, at least functional and partly beneficial to the children and families directly involved, given the socio-economic circumstances of the community in question. It is too simple and too easily subject to counter attack to condemn child work *per se.*

Standing argues Convention No.138 is an obvious example of an over-generalised instrument. However, the International Labour Organisation claims that it does not forbid all forms of child work, for example work within the family circle should be allowed, it only seeks to forbid child work that demand high mental and physical effort that children do not normally possess (Bouhdiba, 1982:33). However, in the long run the International Labour Organisation still wishes to abolish child labour internationally.

This study shows that the International Labour Organisation's effort to identify types of child work or child work in different sectors of the economy that is harmful or hazardous to children, than to prohibit or regulate them, is very important but inadequate. Often the negative impact of child work may be unrelated to the nature and condition of child work. Besides, this study also shows that family work, which is regarded as acceptable by the International Labour Organisation, can be as detrimental (or even more detrimental) as non-family work. It is interesting that often all forms of child work have both positive and negative impact on children; the difference is in the degree of each.

We must also realise that "law by itself is only one component of a large set of policy instruments and usually cannot and is not used by itself" (Dror, Undated:2). For example, if those who drop out of school were not allowed to work, they would have to stay idle. Many Chinese will find this unacceptable. To them child labour may be evil but staying idle is a greater evil for children, as it may encourage them to be lazy, which is against the Chinese culture. To solve the problem a package of policy instruments that take into consideration various possible causes of the problem and consequences of intervention must be designed carefully.

A policy dealing with the root of the problem is more effective than a simple prohibition, although a simple prohibition would be more effective than the present law. We have seen that many full-time child workers go to work because they drop out of school due to poor performance or because of disciplinary problems. If they are not allowed to work this problem of child labour may simply transform into other forms of social problems. Therefore, a more effective way of controlling full-time child labour is to reform the education system to help the weaker students and to prevent children from becoming delinquent. The Education Ministry's plan to set up remedial classes for weak pupils in the primary schools (*New Straits Times*, 3 September 1998) and to work out a new curriculum to help weak secondary students (*New Straits Times*, 4 September 1998) are long overdue. Besides the recent decision to allow those who sit for the PMR (Penilaian Menengah Rendah) to be promoted to Form 4 regardless of their result and the low achievers will be eligible for a place in vocational schools, should be welcomed (*New Straits Times*, 31 December 1998).

We must also be very careful with the message that the law and other policy instruments are sending to the public. We have seen from above that the effectiveness of the law can be influenced by public perception of the law. This is an important consideration if the law or other policy instruments are to be effective. For example, the international instruments often emphasise the rights of children. When this is communicated to the Chinese, it is difficult for them to understand its significance or to accept it. The Chinese are normally paternalistic and pragmatic. Besides, the concept of "individual rights" is of minimum importance in Chinese culture, especially in the parent-child relationship. When we tell them that their children have a right not to work and a right to play, many may probably resist the idea. However, if they are told that their children need to receive more education, and this is good for their children's future achievement in their career, and it is their responsibility as parents to see that their children receive enough education, they are more likely to agree. This is because in the Chinese culture, parent-child relationship is governed by the concept "*Xiao*". *Xiao* places a responsibility on parents to produce children that glorify their ancestors; and being educated or successful is a way of glorifying the ancestors. This is evidenced in many interviews with the parents. They often agree or disagree with child labour on the count of their children's education[18] and career.

Finally, the enforcement agency must be suitable. It is clear in this study that child labour is not purely a labour problem. Child labour is a complex social and cultural problem. Its impact goes far beyond economic losses; they include social, educational, moral, psychological (self-esteem) and physical impact on children. The Labour Department is clearly not a suitable agency to enforce the law. A better agency to deal with this complex problem is probably the Welfare Department because child labour should be seen as a form of social rather than labour problem.

Some Recommendations

After considering some principles of effective policymaking on child labour, it is time to make some concrete recommendations. The writer is aware that the following recommendations will not solve all the problems caused by child labour, however it is hoped that they will at least be much more effective as compared to the present policy in Malaysia. Some international instruments should be adopted, if appropriate. The principles discussed above will be followed if it is possible.

Legal Policy

It is recommended that the law should concentrate on preventing full-time child work. Full-time child work causes the most problems, yet it is the easiest to control.

---

[18] As was indicated in Chapter 5, child work is often seen as a way to educate children. On the other hand, it is the responsibility of parents to ensure their children's wellbeing.

The simplest way to control full-time child work is to prevent children from dropping out of school. Compulsory education up to Form 3 should be introduced as recommended by the International Labour Organisation's Convention No.138, together with some reforms in the education system. If children are kept in school, naturally there will not be full-time child worker. Besides, compulsory education will be relatively easier to enforce, as at present enrolment in primary school is good at least for the Chinese. Once the children are enrolled they should not be allowed to drop out. However, the education system needs to be reformed to cater for the needs of the weaker students.

Part-time child workers should be protected against exploitative or harmful child work as a form of child abuse. Child abuse has already gained enough publicity and recognition in our society as a social problem. Defining certain types of child labour as child abuse has the advantage of ensuring that measures against child labour are more effective. Therefore, besides its coercive function, the law also performs an educational function. However, we should study carefully what kind of child work should be defined as child abuse. Nevertheless, when there is work accident involving a child, the person whom the child works for should be made liable for the accident and must be deemed as having committed an offence. No employment contract is needed. Since the person whom the child works for is, to some extent, in control of the child's work, he should be liable for any damage done to the child. The emphasis should be on the parents and the employers' responsibility to the child, rather than the rights of the child. This measure will ensure that children at work are properly insured against the risks. The cost of hiring children will thus increase, and some employers will be discouraged to hire children.

Education

Compulsory education will not be effective if it is not coupled with a reform to the education system. The current Malaysian education system gives too much emphasis on good students and allows weak students to drop out easily.

According to a recent study commissioned by YB Dato' Hon Choon Kim, the present Deputy Minister of Education under the *No One Less movement*, about 24.48% of the Chinese students in the country drop out of schools before completing their secondary education (一个不能少, 2005). Various factors are sited; most of them correspond with the findings of this study (徐云彪, 2004:97-106). The 24.48% dropout rate is certainly too high after so many years of economic development. As such more attention should be devoted to the weak students. This emphasis is in line with the Vision 2020, to create a developed and a caring society. In a developed nation we need a large skilled labour force, which need to be trained. Besides, concern for the people's educational need is an important feature of a caring society, as education is an important means to ensure a person's welfare in a modern society.

It is recommended that vocational education should be introduced earlier, immediately after children finish primary school. In the present system many weak students have to drop out of school before they are given an opportunity to opt for vocational education. Perhaps we may refer to the streaming system in Singapore, where students are streamed into technical and academic stream much earlier. The school authority may also co-operate with the industry, to send students to work in the industry as part of their course. This arrangement may help to reduce cost of running vocational education and make courses more practical. However, how this new system should work is beyond the scope of this study. More in-depth study is needed to design a workable system.

There are two type of school system that we may also consider, i.e. the Street School system in the United States of America and the Gong Du schools (工读学校) in China.

The first Street School is founded by Tom Tillapaugh in 1984, in Denver, USA. The Denver Street School caught the attention of many educators. Subsequently many similar schools are founded throughout America. In 1996, Tom Tillapaugh again founded the National Association of Street School acting as a coordinator among the Street Schools.[19]

The Street School is founded as an alternative to juvenile reform centres. Tom Tallapaugh found that many juvenile reforms fail because juvenile in the reform centres form an inferiority complex, and subsequently go back to their old life style due to the stigma attached to them after the reform.

The mission of Street School is to accept students dropped out of schools due to marginal activities, give them personal attention, reform their characters through various religious activities, and than prepare them to acquire a high school certificate. Hopefully, the students will acquire a sense of self-confidence to lead a normal and fruitful life afterwards.

---

[19] Interested readers may refer to the association's website at *http://www.streetschool.com*

Over the years, the Street School system has achieved much success; many graduates have got into universities, the army and industry.[20]

On the other hand, Gong Du School (车炜坚, 1996:155-166) accepts students with mild delinquency; it is a type of vocational school that allows student to study and work at the same time. Its mission is to reform delinquent children into one with inspirations, characters, discipline and cultured; subsequently a contributing member of society.

Gong Du School stressed on discipline and character building. Usually boys and girls are separated, male and female teachers are assigned to take care of students of the same gender. The students will first go through a period of discipline and character building before they learn vocational skills. At the later stage of their schooling, they will begin to work in the factory founded by the school.

Although Gong Du School stressed on discipline, there is usually no fence at the school. The schools are as beautiful as a garden. Members of the public, Old boys and girls are often invited to share with students their experience and values.

Schooling in Gong Du Schools is divided into three stages:

1. **Adaptation Stage**
   At this stage students will be made to understand that Gong Du School is not a reform centre. The school does not see them as criminals. They will also be introduced the school rules and regulation. When they begin to

---

[20] Interested readers may refer to the Denver Street School's website at *http://www.denverstreetschool.com*

understand that their teachers do care for them, they will usually settle down. This usually takes about three months.

2. **Reversal Stage**

   This is the most important stage. Much long acquired behaviour will have to be "reversed" and unlearned; and many characters must be learned during this stage. It is not easy of course to change long-acquired habits. Therefore, the process has to be repeated again and again. Character building, inspiration instillation and discipline will be introduced during this stage too. Later at this stage, the students will begin learning useful skills and work in the factory.

3. **Confirmation Stage**

   Before students leave the school, they will go through a revision of what they have learnt in the school. They will be reminded of the aspirations and values they acquired, hopefully they will treasure them.

Street Schools and Gong Du Schools are similar in the sense that they both try to reform their students through discipline, counselling and care. Classes are relatively small so that teachers can give personal attention to their students. Both of them also emphasise on building the self-esteem of their students.

The present writer thinks that it is important to have alternative school system like the above to accept weaker students. The Education Department should also conduct serious study on how to deal with delinquent students. Expulsion and suspension from school will not solve the problem but exacerbate it.

Raising Awareness

We have seen the importance of parental attitudes as a determinant of child work. Attitudes are difficult to change by force, although some element of force is necessary. Besides enforcing the new laws, there should also be some programmes to raise awareness about the negative impact of child work and the importance of education and good parenting. The writer believes raising awareness is very important to reduce the problems of child labour because as shown in Chapter 5, parents who are more educated are less likely to send or allow their children to work. Since they are more aware of the potential negative impact of child work, they are less keen to send or allow their children to work, unless they are sure that their children are doing work that is beneficial.

Child work should not be condemned *per se*. Instead parents and the public should be educated about the physical capacity and development of children in simple terms, so that children are not required to do work that is harmful to them. The public should be informed about the law clearly so that there is no misunderstanding that all forms of child work are illegal, because as this study has shown, this misunderstanding can further condemn some child workers who are already exploited. For example, it may deny them their rightful fringe benefits and legal right to take action against their employers when accident happens at work.

The public should be encouraged to report cases of abuse. This can be done by including the negative impact of child labour together in the campaign against child abuse. Child abuse has gained much publicity in this country and is more accepted by the society as a social problem.

Bibliography

Abdul Rahim, **I.**, "Child Labour: the Law and Its Enforcement in Malaysia." *Journal of the Malaysian Society of Health*, 11(1), 1993:11-19.

Abd Rahman, **R.**, "Child Labour in Malaysia: a General Legal Perspective." *Business Law Journal*, 1, 1996:xcvi-cx.

Aubert, **V.**, "Some Social Functions of Legislation." In Vilhelm Aubert (Ed.), *Sociology of Law*. Penguins, 1969.

Bekomobo, **M.**, "The Child in Africa: Socialisation, Education and Work." Rodgers, G. and Standing, G. (ed.), *Child Work, Poverty and Underdevelopment*. Geneva: International Labour Office (ILO), 1981.

Bequele, **A.**, "Child Labour: Question and Answers", International Labour Office, *Child Labour: A Briefing Manual*. Geneva: International Labour Office, 1986.

Bequele, A. and **M.E. Myers**, *First Things First in Child Labour-Eliminating Work Detrimental to Children*. Geneva: International Labour Office (ILO), 1995.

Blanchard, F., "Child Labour: The ILO Perspective." In International Labour Office, *Child Labour: A Briefing Manual*. Geneva: 1986.

Bouhdiba, A., *Exploitation of Child Labour*. New Yoke: United Nations, 1982.

Chan, **Paul**, "The Forgotten Little People: Urban Child Labour in Metropolitan Malaysia." In K.S. Jomo (Ed.), *Child Labour in Malaysia*. Malaysia: Forum, 1992:132-143.

Clammer, **J.**, Fishermen, "Forest-eaters, Peddlers, Peasants, and Pastoralists: Economic Anthropology." In G. Evans (Ed.), *Asian's*

Cultural Mosaic: An Anthropological Introduction. Singapore: Prentice Hall, 1993.

Cotterrell, R., *The Sociology of Law: An Introduction.* London: Butterworths, 1984.

Dennis De Tray, "Children's Work Activities in Malaysia." *Population and Development Review,* 9(3), 1983:437-455.

Doek, E., "Ways and Means of Achieving Elimination of the Exploitation of child Labour in All Parts of the World." *Conference on Child Labour and Child Prostitution.* Kuala Lumpur: 1986.

Dube, L., "The Economic Roles of Children in India: Methodological Issues." In G. Rodgers and G. Standing (Ed.), *Child Work, Poverty and Underdevelopment.* Geneva: International Labour Office (ILO), 1981.

Dror, Y., *Law as a Tool of Directed Social Change: A framework for Policymaking.* (Photocopy in University Malaya Law Library).

Forastieri, V., *Children at Work: Health and Safety Risks.* Geneva: International Labour office, 1997.

Fyfe, A. and **M. Jankanish**, *Trade Unions and Child Labour.* Geneva: International Labour Office, 1997.

George, M., "Children in Employment in Peninsular Malaysia." In K.S. Jomo (Ed.), *Child Labour in Malaysia.* Malaysia: Forum, 1992:1-75.

Grossfield, B., *The Strength and Weakness of Comparative Law.* Oxford: Clarendon Press, 1990:41-49.

Hull, T., "Perspective and Data Requirements for the Study of Children's Work". In G. Rodgers and G. Standing (Ed.), *Child Work, Poverty and Underdevelopment.* Geneva: International Labour office (IL)), 1981.

International Labour Office, *Child Labour: A Briefing Manual.* Geneva: International Labour Office, 1986.

International Labour Office, *Child Labour: Targeting the Intolerable.* Geneva: International Labour Office, 1996.

Jain, M.P., "Child Labour in Malaysia." In C. Hongladrom and Phaisith (Ed.), *Asian Regional Congress of Labour Law and Social Security.* Bangkok: 1985.

Jensen Report, Development of Indicators on Child Labour. http://www.ilo.org/public/english/standards/ipec/simpoz/jensen/page1.htm.

Jillani, A., "Child Exploitation in Pakistan." *Malaysian Law News*. September 1993:27-30.

Jomo, K.S., J. **Zaini**, R. **Ramasamy** and S. **Suppiah**, "Early Labour: Children at Work on Malaysian Plantations." In K.S. Jomo (Ed.), *Child Labour in Malaysia*. Malaysia: Forum, 1992:144-171.

Krishnapillai, S., "Child Labour in Malaysia." In C. Chirahongladarom and Phaisith (Ed.), *Asian Regional Congress of Labour Law and Social Security*. Bangkok: 1985.

Lai Ah-Eng, "Child Labour in Small-Scale Industries in Penang." In K.S. Jomo (Ed.), *Child Labour in Malaysia*. Malaysia: Forum: 1992:112-131.

Lin, **Chin-Yau Cindy** and **Victoria R. Fu**, "A Comparison of Child-rearing Practice Among Chinese, Immigrant Chinese, and Caucasian-American Parents." *Child Development*, 61, 1990:429-433.

Mahathevan, R., "Special Risk Factors of Children at Work in Penisular Malaysia." In K.S. Jomo (Ed.), *Child Labour in Malaysia*. Malaysia: Forum: 1992:76-111.

Mohamud, S., "Child Labour in Malaysia: an Overview from Legal Aspect." *Conference on Child Labour and Child Prostitution*. Kuala Lumpur: 1986.

Nyce, **Ray**, *Chinese New Village in Malaysia: A Community Study*. Malaysian Sociological Research Institute, 1973.

Podgorecki, A., *Law and Society*. Routledge & Kegan Paul., 1974.

Rodgers, G., and G. **Standing** (Ed.), *Child Work, Poverty and Underdevelopment*. Geneva: International Labour Office (ILO), 1981.

Rodgers, G. and G. **Standing**, "The Economic Roles of Children: Issues for Analysis." In Rodgers, G. and Standing, G. (Ed.), *Child Work, Poverty and Underdevelopment*. Geneva: International Labour Office (ILO), 1981a.

Rodgers, H.R. and C.S. **Bullock**, *Law and Social Change: Civil Rights Laws and Their Consequences*. McGraw-Hill Book Co., 1972.

Schildkrout, E., “The Employment of Children in Kano.” In G. Rodgers and G. Standing (Ed.), *Child Work, Poverty and Underdevelopment.* Geneva: International Labour Office (ILO), 1981.

Shipman, **M.D.**, *Childhood: A Sociological Perspective.* NFER Publishing Company Ltd., 1972.

Sim Sock Hoon, “Confucius’ Tenet of Filial Piety and Its Justifications.” *Asian Culture*, 4, 1984:80-84.

Sinniah, B., “Support for the Working Child.” *National Seminar on Working Children in Malaysia.* Kuala Lumpur: 1993.

Sinniah and **B. Rajeswari**, “Child Labour-High Risk for Abuse.” *Journal of the Malaysian Society of Health*, 11(1), 1993:21-26.

Sorensen, **C.W.**, “Asian Families: Domestic Group Formation.” In G. Evans (Ed.), *Asia’s Cultural Mosaic – An Anthropological Introduction.* New York: Prentice Hall, 1993.

Standing, **G.**, “State Policy and Child Labour: Accumulation Versus Legitimation?” *Development and Change*, 13(4) October 1982:611-631.

Swepton, **L.**, “Child Labour: Its Regulation by ILO Standards and National Legislation.” In International Labour Office, *Child Labour: A Briefing Manual.* Geneva: International Labour Office, 1986.

Tai Hung-Chao, “Measuring the Economic Impact of Confucianism: Surveys of Chinese and Americans’ Attitudes Toward Education and Savings.” *Asian Culture*, 18, 1994:6-28.

Tengku Bot, **T.O.**, Keynote Address. *National Seminar on Working Children in Malaysia.* Kuala Lumpur: 1993.

Wu Ming Chu, *Culture, Social Organisation and Economic Activities of a Chinese Farming Community: A case Study in Skinchang, Selangor, Malaysia* (Unpublished PhD Thesis). Kuala Lumpur: University Malaya: 1995.

Yaqin, A., *Law and Society in Malaysia.* Kuala Lumpur: International Law Book Services, 1996:155-164.

Yen Ching-Hwang, “Class Structure and Social Mobility in the Chinese Community in Singapore and Malaya, 1800-1911.” *Community and Politics: The Chinese in Colonial Singapore and Malaysia.* Time Academic Press, 1995.

Zaini, J., "Child Labour in Malaysian Plantations." *Conference on Child Labour and Child Prostitution*. Kuala Lumpur: 1986.

References in Chinese

侯家驹, 儒家思想与经济发展及其对台湾经济的贡献, *Chinese Social Science Quarterly*, Summer, 1993:162-175.

何子煌, «孝经» 内容分析, *亚洲文化*, 1983:32£-39.

金耀基, 个人与社会：儒家伦理典范的特性及在其现代社会中的问题, 资料与研究 1994:28-37.

崔贵强, 战后新加坡华人家庭的变异, 资料与研究, 1994:67-69.

徐云彪, 华裔中学生辍学的一些研究, *心叙神游*, 大将出版社, 2004:97-106.

车炜坚, *香港青少年犯罪问题*, 中华书局, 1996:155-166.

Official Reports

The Seventh Malaysia Plan 1996-2000, 1997:70-74.

Newspapers

"Labour's Lost Innocents", *Star*, 1 May 1994.

"Children Belong to Parents", *Nanyang Siang Pau*, 6 May 1994.

"Children Who Work Prone to Poor Health", *Star*, 8 September 1994.

"雇用童工, 超时工作 — 芙电子厂罚俞万元", *Sin Chew Jit Poh*, 15 December 1994.

"Tiada Maaf Pelajar Terlibat Kongsi Gelap", *Utusan Melayu*, 26 June 1995.

"近 1%学生逃学"，*Nanyang Siang Pau*, 30 November 1995.

"Bosses May Have to Register Minor", *Star*, 6 December 1995.

"Pupils Skip Classes to Make Fast Buck", *New Straits Times*, 30 January 1996.

"华人唯一保留地-无拉港工业区致力规划现代化", *Nanyang Siang Pau*, 11 October 1996.

"Assemblyman Wants Progress in Balakong", *New Straits Times*, 25 August 1997.

"Bangla Balakong", *Harian Metro*, 28 October 1997.

"Illegal Video-arcade Operators hire Gangsters to Scare Exco Official", *Star*, 18 November 1997.

"Remedial Classes For Weak Pupils", *New Straits Times*, 3 September 1998.

"Syllabus Planned For Weak Students", *New Straits Times*, 4 September 1998.

"Minimum 11 Years Education For All", *New Straits Times*, 31 December 1998.